EMOTI INTELLIGENCE

Mastery

The Best Guide to Improving Your Social Skills, Your Confidence, Have a Better Life and Relationships, Success at Work, and Discover Why it Can Matter More Than IQ

DR. JOSHUA MILLER

bng-books.com

BNG
Books

Acknowledgment

I want to thank you for buying my book and for trusting in me, sincerely ...Thanks!

Writing a book is harder than I thought and more rewarding than I could have ever imagined.

My thanks go to all of you, readers, I thank you because without you I could not be what I am, without you my books simply…would not exist!

I would like to introduce you all my works, and, if you like them, invite you to leave a positive thought; this will help me to continue my work and will help other people to buy what they are looking for!

Again…Thanks You!

Dr. Joshua Miller

Click to see all my books

bng-books.com

TABLE OF CONTENTS

Introduction

The workplace no longer needs to linger in the dark about the factors that lead to great performance. More than 25 years of neurological research and specific studies on the factors that contribute to workplace success have led to revolutionary perceptions of intelligence. Quantifiable data on performance across a myriad of industries and organizations has produced a body of study called emotional intelligence. These years of study have named and identified the "intangibles" that predict success in the workplace. Emotional intelligence explains why, despite the same intellectual ability, training, or experience, some people excel while others of the same caliber lag behind.

Time and again, we have heard and told stories of people with intellectual brilliance often coupled with great experience and education that have not always produced the most capable leaders. Sometimes, even worse, these purveyors of knowledge and intellect created emotional disasters among their followers and plagued the halls of American corporations by condemning their followers to a working life of little creativity, minimal enthusiasm, low productivity and even fear. And, of course, the corporate response was "send them to a training course". The training lessons almost always fell short because the training was not designed to get to the root of the matter and develop the core question. Furthermore, the training was generically designed and was not aimed at the individual's bankruptcy prescription.

The brilliant research of Daniel Goleman, Robert Cooper, Ayman Sawaf and Robert Kelley quantified the characteristics of emotional intelligence and enabled measurement in a field that previously lacked such measurement and definition. It is no longer a "case" that certain skills are repeatedly found in high performance subjects. Many of these skills are found in high-performing companies at all levels, from customer service representatives to CEOs. It is no longer the discussion on non-quantifiable "soft skills". Instead, we as trainers and coaches have to find ways to build those talents that have been identified by these experts and labeled as emotional intelligence.

CHAPTER1

EMOTIONAL INTELLIGENCE (EI)

What Is It?

The concept of emotional intelligence (named EI as an acronym) is relatively recent; in fact, the first definition dates back to 1990 and was proposed by the American psychologists Peter Salovey and John D. Mayer.

The transformations undergone by the concept of emotional intelligence over the years have led to the creation by psychologists and scholars of the sector of different theoretical models of EI, corresponding to equally different definitions and characteristics. Throughout the article, the models proposed first by Salovey and Mayer and then by Goleman will be taken into consideration, highlighting their characteristics and peculiarities.

Emotional intelligence can be described as the ability of an individual to recognize, discriminate and identify, to label appropriately and, consequently, to manage their emotions and those of others in order to achieve certain goals.

In truth, the definition of emotional intelligence has undergone several changes over the years and its meaning can take on different shades depending on the type of conception that people have of this ability to identify and manage their own and others' emotions.

Emotional intelligence is also known as emotional quotient (named EQ as an acronym), emotional intelligence quotient (EIQ) and emotional leadership (EL).

As mentioned, the conception of emotional intelligence is not univocal, but there are several theoretical models proposed that describe its meaning and characteristics. Below are two of the main models of emotional intelligence currently in existence: that of Salovey and Mayer and that of Goleman.

Emotional Intelligence According to Salovey and Mayer

The concept of emotional intelligence initially developed by psychologists Salovey and Mayer defined it as the ability to perceive, integrate and regulate emotions to facilitate thought and promote personal growth.

However, after conducting several researches, this definition was changed to include the ability to accurately perceive emotions, to generate and understand them so as to reflexively regulate them in order to promote one's emotional and intellectual growth.

More specifically, according to the Salovey and Mayer model, emotional intelligence includes four different skills:

- perception of emotions: the perception of emotions is a fundamental aspect of emotional intelligence. In this case, it is understood as the ability to detect and decipher not only one's emotions, but also those of others, on people's faces, in images (for example, in photographs), in the timbre of the voice, etc.;
- use of emotions: it is understood as the individual's ability to exploit emotions and apply them to activities such as thinking and solving problems;
- understanding of emotions: it is the ability to understand emotions and to understand their variations and evolution over time;
- managing emotions: consists of the ability to regulate one's own and others' emotions, both positive and negative, managing them in such a way as to achieve the set goals.

According to Salovey and Mayer the above abilities are closely related to each other.

How Is Emotional Intelligence Measured According to Salovey and Mayer?

The degree of emotional intelligence according to the Salovey and Mayer model is measured by the Mayer-Salovey-Caruso emotional intelligence test (also known by the acronym of MSEIT). Without going into details, we will limit ourselves to saying that this test verifies the individual on the aforementioned abilities that characterize emotional intelligence. Unlike the classic IQ tests, in the MSEIT there are no objectively correct answers; this feature, however, has largely contributed to questioning the reliability of the test itself.

Emotional Intelligence According to Goleman

According to the model introduced by Goleman, emotional intelligence encompasses a series of skills and competences that guide the individual especially in the field of leadership. In detail, according to Goleman, emotional intelligence is characterized by:

- self-awareness: it is understood as the ability to recognize one's emotions and strengths, as well as one's limits and weaknesses. It also includes the ability to understand how these personal characteristics are able to influence others;
- self-regulation: describes the ability to manage one's strengths, emotions and weaknesses, adapting them to the different situations that may arise, in order to achieve goals and objectives;
- social skill: consists of the ability to manage relationships with people in order to "direct" them towards achieving a certain goal;
- motivation: it is the ability to recognize negative thoughts and transform them into positive thoughts that are able to motivate oneself and others;

- empathy: it is the ability to fully understand and even perceive and feel the mood of other people.

According to Goleman, different emotional skills belong to each of the aforementioned characteristics, understood as the practical skills of the individual necessary for the establishment of positive relationships with others. These skills, however, are not innate, but can be learned, developed and improved in order to achieve important job and leadership performance. According to Goleman, each individual is endowed with "general" emotional intelligence from birth and the degree of this intelligence determines the - more or less high - probability of later learning and exploiting the above emotional skills.

Goleman, therefore, makes emotional intelligence a fundamental tool in the context of job success.

How Is Emotional Intelligence Measured According to Goleman?

Goleman's emotional intelligence can be measured through the Emotional Competency Inventory (ECI) and the Emotional and Social Competency Inventory (ESCI), these are tools developed by Goleman himself and by Richard Eleftherios Boyatzis, professor of organizational behavior, psychology and cognitive sciences.

Furthermore, it is also possible to measure emotional intelligence through the Emotional Intelligence Appraisal. It is a type of self-assessment developed by Travis Bradberry and Jean Greaves.

Effects and Benefits of Emotional Intelligence on Daily Life

Regardless of the type of model adopted to describe traits and characteristics, the presence of a high degree of emotional intelligence - understood as the ability to perceive, recognize and correctly manage one's own and others' emotions - should theoretically bring beneficial effects in all aspects of the individual's daily life.

In detail, those with emotional intelligence should:
- have better social relationships;
- have better family and romantic relationships;
- be perceived by others in a more positive way than individuals with low emotional intelligence;
- be able to establish better relationships in the workplace than those who do not have, or have a low level of emotional intelligence;
- be more likely to understand people and make correct decisions based on both logic and emotions;
- have a better academic performance;
- enjoy greater psychological well-being.

Those with a good level of emotional intelligence, in fact, seem to have a greater chance of getting satisfaction from their life, having a high level of self-esteem and a lower level of insecurity. Furthermore, the presence of emotional intelligence seems to be useful in preventing wrong choices and behaviors, also related to one's health (for example, abuse of psychoactive substances and addictions to both drugs and alcohol).

Curiosity

An interesting study conducted in 2010 analyzed the correlation between emotional intelligence and the degree of addiction to alcohol and/or drugs. From this study it emerged that the scores obtained from the tests for the evaluation of emotional intelligence increased as the degree of dependence on the aforementioned substances decreased.

The same goes for another study conducted in 2012 that analyzed the relationship between emotional intelligence, self-esteem and marijuana addiction: subjects affected by this addiction scored exceptionally low on tests of both evaluation and self-esteem, as well as emotional intelligence tests.

Criticisms

There are many criticisms of the concept of emotional intelligence. Only a few will be reported below.

Measurement of Emotional Intelligence

One of the main criticisms advanced against emotional intelligence concerns the inability to measure it objectively. Although tests are available for its measurement both according to the Salovey and Mayer model, and according to the Goleman model, many doubt their reliability, as not exactly objective since there are no objectively correct or incorrect answers.

Between Saying and Doing

Remaining in the context of the methods used to measure emotional intelligence and the doubts about the reliability of the tests used to determine its degree, a new criticism emerges, namely that what emerges from them is not always true.

Indeed, the fact that from the execution of the aforementioned tests it emerges that a person knows how to manage emotions and how to behave accordingly in a certain situation, even a critical one, does not necessarily mean that that person reacts in that way (emerged from the test) when that person certain situation arises.

Utility of Emotional Intelligence

Another criticism - especially against Goleman's interpretation - concerns the real usefulness of having a high emotional intelligence in the workplace. According to Goleman, in fact, a high emotional intelligence increases the probability of job success, especially at the executive level. The criticisms leveled in this regard affirm that a greater ability to recognize and identify one's own and others' emotions does not always lead to success, but rather can put the leader in difficulty, who must make important decisions. The studies conducted on the subject do not deny but do not even confirm this criticism. In fact, from the studies published so far, it has emerged that in some situations a high emotional intelligence is helpful in achieving work success, in others it is neutral and in still others it can be counterproductive. This is because, the ability to succeed does not only depend on the degree of emotional intelligence, but also on the IQ, on the personality of the individual and on the working role that it covers.

Tool to Achieve Goals or Weapon of Manipulation?

Finally, we report a final criticism concerning the fact that emotional intelligence is considered by almost everyone as a desirable trait.

In this sense, the idea has been advanced that not always the ability to manage the emotions of others to achieve certain goals can be considered as a positive aspect, since this ability could be misused as a "weapon" to manipulate thought and the action of others in their favor.

Regardless of the model considered, the definition of emotional intelligence, the methods and tests by which it is measured, and even its very existence, are still being questioned. According to some, in fact, there would be no emotional intelligence understood as a type of intelligence in its own right, but the ability to recognize, identify, label and manage one's own emotions and those of others would be nothing more than intelligence applied to a particular domain of life, namely that of emotions.

The concept of emotional intelligence, therefore, still remains the subject of much debate.

What Emotional Intelligence Is NOT

In the light of what has been said so far, it is clear that there is no single definition of emotional intelligence and how its meaning and its applications can change according to the theoretical models taken into consideration. It is not surprising, therefore, that the concept of emotional intelligence is often distorted and/or misunderstood and that irrelevant meanings are attributed to it. In this regard, the same psychologist John D. Mayer wanted to spend a few words in an article published in an American trade magazine to specify that - contrary to what can be read in numerous articles and magazines - emotional intelligence is NOT synonymous with happiness, optimism, calm and self-control, since these are traits that may or may not belong to the personality of the individual and must not be "mixed" with the characteristics and abilities attributed to emotional intelligence.

CHAPTER 2

EMOTIONS

Without emotion, time is just a clock ticking...

Emotions exert an incredibly powerful force on human behavior. Strong emotions can cause actions that you wouldn't normally do. But what exactly are emotions? What triggers these reactions? I wanted to briefly summarize some of the main theories of emotions that have been proposed by researchers, philosophers and psychologists.

Definition of Emotion

Emotion is understood as the set of organic reactions that an individual experiences when responding to certain external stimuli that allow him to adapt to a situation with respect to a person, an object, a place, among others.

The word emotion comes from the Latin Emotion, which means "movement", "impulse".

Emotion is characterized by being a short-term mood alteration but of greater intensity than a sensation. On the other hand, feelings are the consequences of emotions, which is why they are more lasting and can be verbalized.

Emotions are the cause of various organic reactions that can be physiological, psychological or behavioral, that is, they are reactions that can be both innate and influenced by previous experiences or knowledge.

These organic reactions that generate emotions are controlled by the limbic system, made up of various brain structures that control physiological responses. However, an emotion can also produce a behavior that can be learned in advance, such as a facial expression.

Furthermore, Charles Darwin hypothesized that facial expressions convey various emotions which, in general, are very similar in all human beings. He also established that emotional behaviors evolve based on their postures or movements.

On the other hand, there are other theories on emotion also framed in the Physiology, Psychology or behavior of humans and animals. Among the most important theories are those made by James-Lange, Cannon-Bard, Schachter-Singer, James Papez, among others.

However, it should also be remembered the Affective Neuroscience, a term given by JA Panksepp, that is a branch of neuroscience that is responsible for the study of the neurological components of emotions, affective processes and mood not only in humans, but also in the animals.

What Are Emotions in Psychology?

Emotions in Psychology are often defined as a complex state of feelings that result in physical and psychological changes that affect thinking and behavior. Emotionality is associated with a series of psychological phenomena including temperament, personality, mood and motivation. According to author David G. Meyers, human emotion involves "... physiological arousal, expressive behavior, and conscious experience."

The Theories on Emotions
The main theories can be grouped into three main categories: physiological, neurological and cognitive.

Physiological theories suggest that the responses within our body are responsible for feelings.
Neurological theories propose that activity inside the brain leads to emotional responses.
Cognitive theories hold that thoughts and other mental activities play an essential role in the formation of emotional states.

The James-Lange Theory
The James-Lange theory is one of the best known examples of a physiological theory of emotions. Psychologist William James and physiologist Carl Lange, independently of each other, proposed similar theories on emotion. They both wanted to challenge what they called the common sense theory that when someone is asked "why are you crying?" he replies: "because I'm sad".
This response implies the belief that sensations come first, which, in turn, produce the physiological and expressive aspects of emotion.

According to James and Lange, we must fight the theory of common sense, since we do not cry because we are sad, but we feel sad because we cry; we do not tremble because we are afraid, but we feel fear because we are trembling. The heart does not beat faster because we are angry, but we are angry because the heart beats faster.

The emotional reaction depends on how the physical reactions are interpreted.

The Cannon-Bard Theory

Walter Cannon in 1927published a critique of the James-Lange theory which convinced many psychologists that it was an unsustainable theory.

Cannon, pointed out that research had by no means shown that emotion is accompanied by a single physiological event. The same general state of sympathetic nervous system activation is present in many different emotions.

For example, the visceral states that accompany fear and anger are exactly the same that are associated with feelings of cold and fever. It does not therefore seem possible that physiological modifications in the visceral organs cause recognizable differentiated emotional states.

This hypothesis was later elaborated by Philip Bard (1929), according to whom the thalamus plays a critical role in the emotional experience. For Cannon and Bard (Cannon - Bard theory), the nerve impulses that pass sensory information are then retransmitted through the thalamus. By receiving this input upwards from the cortex (causing a subjective emotional experience) and downwards to the muscles, glands and visceral organs (producing physiological changes).

The Schachter-Singer Theory

Also known as the two-factor theory of emotion, the Schachter-Singer Theory is an example of a cognitive theory of emotion. This theory suggests that physiological arousal occurs first, and then the individual must identify the reason for this excitement to experience and label it as an emotion.

Do cognitive or emotional processes come first?

In the past few years, two theories have been put forward about normal emotional experiences. These are theories that pay relatively little attention to the role of biological modifications and physiological activation. The controversy currently centers on which comes first, whether cognitive assessment or subjective sensations.

According to the theory of cognitive evaluation, the sequence of events first involves a stimulus, then a thought, to lead to the simultaneous experience of a physiological response and emotion. For example, if you encounter a large boar in the woods, you immediately realize that you could be in great danger. Here comes the emotional experience, that is, that of fear and the physical reactions associated with the fight or flight reaction.

Which Are the Main Emotions?

There are two types of emotions:

- the core emotions;
- complex emotions.

The fundamentals are also called primary emotions as they occur in the initial periods of human life and unite us to many other animal species. The newborn shows three fundamental emotions that are defined as "innate":

- fear;
- love;
- anger.

Within the first five years of life, it manifests other fundamental emotions such as:

- shame;
- anxiety;
- jealousy;
- envy.

Primary Emotions List

- Anger. Generated by frustration and can manifest itself through aggression;
- Fear. It is an emotion dominated by instinct, it has as its objective the survival of the subject in a dangerous situation;
- Sadness. It originates as a result of a loss or an unfulfilled goal;
- Joy. It is a positive feeling of those who believe all their desires are satisfied;

- Surprise. It originates from an unexpected event, followed by fear or joy;
- Disgust. Repulsive response characterized by a specific facial expression of this emotion.

Complex (Secondary) Emotions

They are the combination of a primary emotion or more and develop with the growth of the individual and social interaction:

- envy;
- cheerfulness;
- shame;
- anxiety;
- resignation;
- jealousy;
- hope;
- forgiveness;
- offense;
- nostalgia;
- remorse;
- disappointment.

Emotion: What Is It and How Is It Interpreted?

Often people are confused about what an emotion is. They may take feelings too seriously, believing that they are immutable or unavoidable facts. Many try to control emotions by holding on to them or trying to push them away. All these controlling energies make feelings difficult.

If you truly know what emotions are, they can never hurt you or worry you unduly. Stop giving your feelings more power than they really have, understanding what an emotion is and what it isn't.

An emotion is never the "truth" of the moment. A feeling is not reality. Every emotion is your perception of a situation. This doesn't mean that it's not important or that you should ignore how you feel, it just means that you should, at times, take a step back from your feelings. If you feel that they are your answer, you understand that they are not reality. If you feel a certain way, what different perception could you have to feel differently? What are the other aspects of the story?

It is incredible how often we feel enslaved by our emotions, as if a sensation had the power to make us its puppets. Emotions can be powerful, but they cannot move our legs and arms for us, nor open our mouths. We should make our emotions inform us, rather than forcing us to react with a certain action. True wisdom lies in watching your emotions carefully rather than reacting immediately by indulging them immediately.

Although this is certainly not easy, we should keep in mind a teaching of Lao Tse which represents well what I mean; (obviously being able to apply it always, that's all); "Understanding human beings is intelligence, understanding oneself is wisdom".

Every emotionhas a purpose and that is to convey information to us. They can warn us, teach us and tell us what to look out for. Fear, for example, is a suggestion that can serve to protect yourself. Anger is the sign that someone has exceeded your patience. If you listen to the information, you understand why they show up. Acknowledging them deeply allows you to take or avoid sensible actions or not.

It is useful to know that emotions are shared by everyone: they are never only yours. Feelings are part of the human condition. I'm sure that right now, someone else in the world probably feels exactly like you. At any time, we can share the feelings that belong to human beings and feel connected even with just one person in particular. Yet we haven't invented an emotion, we don't have it, and we can't hold it back or keep it for long. You are not an emotion, it is just something you are experiencing at a particular moment in time.

Emotions come and go and never last that long. If you are stuck in pain, anger or sadness, remember that it is actually difficult to sustain an emotion for a certain period of time. You may feel sad or pained for days on end, but if you really think about it, it is probably an emotion that recurs alternately: while taking a walk; when you talk to a friend; while you wash the dishes. And you probably don't feel the way you did yesterday or two weeks ago today. Emotions come and go and for this very reason, you have to let them pass. Sometimes, indulging them too much can block us.

The 12 Laws of Emotions

Professor Nico Frijda has drawn up twelve laws of emotions. Although there are exceptions to every self-respecting law, these guidelines have been summarized after years of psychological research.

1. The situational meaning
The first law says that emotions arise from situations. Generally the same types of situations elicit the same types of emotional response. Loss makes you grieve, gains make you happy, and scary things make you fearful.

2. The law of worry
You are kidnapped by this law when you feel worried about something, when you have a particular interest in what happens, whether it is an object, yourself or another person.

Emotions arise from these particular goals, motivations or concerns. This is the second of the laws of emotions, you suffer every time you are not indifferent to the world around you. After all, how can you worry if you don't feel anything?

3. The law of apparent reality

Whatever feels real to you can elicit an emotional response. In other words, the way you evaluate or interpret a situation governs the emotion you feel (compare with laws 11 and 12). The reason some movies, games, or books don't engage you emotionally is because, in a sense, you can't detect the truth. It's hard to be emotional about things that aren't obvious, and you won't be until they show up in front of you. For example, the news of the loss of a person learned from someone else is much softer emotionally than when you realize that that person you have lost is about to call them on the phone. Now the awareness of the loss of him is very real.

4, 5 & 6. The laws of change, addiction and comparative sentiment

The law of addiction is presented so that in life you get used to the circumstances in which you live, whatever they may be (largely true, but consult laws 7 and 8). Emotions, therefore, respond more easily to change. This means that you continually compare what happens to you to a relatively constant frame of reference (the one you are used to). You get your emotions to respond more easily to changes that are related to this frame of reference.

7. The law of asymmetrical pleasure

There are some terrible circumstances that you never get used to. If things go very badly for you, it is impossible to escape negative feelings such as fear and anxiety. On the other hand, positive emotions always fade with the passage of time. No matter how much in love you are, how big your lottery winnings are, or how good a spree night with friends makes you feel good, positive emotions like the pleasure they give, always slip away.

On the other hand, the famous phrase of Schopenhauer's thought says that: "Human life is like a pendulum that swings incessantly between pain and boredom, passing through the fleeting, and moreover illusory, interval of pleasure and joy".

8. The law of conservation of the emotional moment

Time does not heal all wounds or if it does, it does so only indirectly. Events can retain their emotional power over the years, unless you relive a similar experience that you have reevaluated. It is this re-experimenting and consequent redefinition that reduces the emotional charge of an event. This is why events that have never been reevaluated, for example, having been rejected by a potential lover, retain their emotional power for decades.

9. The law of closure

The way you respond to emotions tends to be absolute. This way leads to drastic actions such as not tolerating any arguments (but see laws 10, 11 and 12). In other words, the emotional responses and therefore those you give without thinking about it for more than a few seconds, are absolutely closing. An emotion takes you and sends you resolutely along a path, until a different emotion directs you to the opposite path.

10. The law of consequences

You can naturally consider the consequences of your emotions and modify your reactions accordingly. For example, anger can trigger violent feelings towards someone else, but generally you refrain from stabbing your interlocutor, like it or not. Maybe to vent your anger you smoke 100 cigarettes in an hour or break your hand by throwing a fist against the wall! Emotions can absolutely dictate a type of response, but people usually try to modulate the size of that response.

11 &12. The laws of the least load and the greatest gain

The emotional impact of an event or situation depends on its interpretation. Try to fake a smile after giving yourself a hammer on your finger. The law of the lesser load says that people are particularly motivated to use re-interpretations to reduce negative emotions. The opposite is also true, that is to evaluate something risky with a negative thought, thus triggering a sense of prudence that helps protect you.

Are the 12 laws of emotions all shareable? One cannot agree with all these "laws", also because the very existence of an emotion is something individual. However, sometimes schematizing the concepts helps to better define the objectives. I think that one of the most difficult goals for each of us to achieve but at the same time the most satisfying is to start living with emotional intelligence.

Primary and Secondary Emotions

Primary emotions, that is, those innate and present in every population, and the secondary ones that originate from the primary ones and arise from social interaction.

Primary emotions are innate emotions and can be found in any population, which is why they are defined as primary or universal. Secondary emotions, on the other hand, are those that originate from the combination of primary emotions and develop with the growth of the individual and with social interaction.

We constantly experience many emotions, a wide range, which varies from positive to negative. Basically, what is an emotion, what is it about? Let's try, therefore, to take a journey into this world, exploring more closely these strangers who accompany us throughout our day and life.

Emotion consists of a series of changes that occur in our body both at the physiological level, respiratory and cardiac alterations, and thoughts, for example: "what a fear" or "there is no hope", and behavioural reactions, such as running away, shouting or alterations in facial expressions, which the subject uses in response to an event.

Surely, if tomorrow there should be a question to be addressed or a written assignment, a verification in short, I could feel anxiety, fear, due to the fact that I do not know how it could go, of not having studied enough, of not knowing exactly which questions will be addressed and what could be the results. In this case, you may feel a number of changes in the body, such as butterflies in the stomach, dry mouth, headache, wheezing and so on. These are indicators concerning the state of uncertainty that is being faced, because the expectations thatpeople have are far from reality.

Many have studied emotions trying to define and categorize them, but today I would like to emphasize the work developed by Ekman in 2008. This American psychologist tells of having been in a remote village on the heights of Papua New Guinea to study the settlements of the place and verify if it was possible to find among them the same emotions felt by other peoples. The indigenous people, the Fore, pre-literary people, were amazed at the sight of Ekman eating something unknown to them. In particular, one of them stood looking at Ekman with a particular expression. The scholar enthusiastic about their reaction, photographed the expression of disgust on the face of this tribe member and wrote: "The photograph illustrates that man is disgusted by the sight and smell of food which I considered appetizing". This is just one of the many examples reported by the scientist.

It was by following this Tribe that Ekman was able to notice how the basic expressions were universal because they can be found in different populations, even in that of the Fore which is isolated from the rest of the world. So he decided to draw up a list of emotions divided into primary and secondary.

Primary or Basic Emotions Are:

1. anger, generated by the frustration that can manifest itself through aggression;
2. fear, emotion dominated by instinct that aims to survive the subject in a dangerous situation;
3. sadness, it originates as a result of a loss or an unfulfilled goal;
4. joy, a positive mood of those who consider all their desires satisfied;
5. surprise, it originates from an unexpected event, followed by fear or joy;
6. contempt, sentiment and attitude of total lack of esteem and disdainful rejection of people or things, considered to have no moral or intellectual dignity;
7. disgust, repulsive response characterized by a specific facial expression.

These are innate emotions and can be found in any population, which is why they are defined as primary or universal.

Secondary Emotions

Secondary emotions, on the other hand, are those that originate from the combination of primary emotions and develop with the growth of the individual and with social interaction.

They are:

- cheerfulness, a feeling of full and lively satisfaction of the soul;
- envy, an emotional state in which a subject feels a strong desire to have what the other has;
- shame, emotional reaction that is felt as a consequence of the transgression of social rules;
- anxiety, emotional reaction due to the foreshadowing of a hypothetical, future and distant danger;
- resignation, disposition of mind of those who patiently accept pain and misfortune;
- jealousy, an emotional state that derives from the fear of losing something that already belongs to the subject;
- hope, tendency to believe that phenomena or events are manageable and controllable and therefore can be addressed towards the best hoped-for results;
- forgiveness, replacement of negative emotions that follow a perceived offense (eg. anger, fear) with positive emotions (eg. empathy, compassion);
- offense, moral damage that is done to a person with deeds or words;
- nostalgia, a state of malaise caused by an acute desire for a distant place, for something or a person absent or lost, for a finished situation that people would like to relive;
- remorse, a state of punishment or psychological disturbance experienced by those who believe they have behaved or acted contrary to their own moral code;
- disappointment, a mood of sadness caused by the realization that the expectations, the hopes cultivated are not reflected in reality.

Thus, the latter are more complex emotions and need more external elements or heterogeneous thoughts to be activated.

Evolution of Our Brain

To better grasp the powerful hold of emotions on the thinking mind - and why feelings and reason are so readily at war - consider how the brain has evolved. Human brains, with their roughly three pounds of cells and neural juices, are about three times that of our closest evolving cousins, non-human primates. Over the course of millions of years of evolution, the brain has grown from the bottom up, with its higher centers developing as elaborations of lower and older parts. (Brain growth in the human embryo more or less retraces this evolutionary course).

The most primitive part of the brain, shared with all species that have more than one minimal nervous system, is the brain stem that surrounds the upper part of the spinal cord. This brain root regulates basic vital functions such as breathing and metabolism of the other organs of the body, as well as controlling stereotyped reactions and movements. This primitive brain cannot be said to think or learn; rather it is a set of preprogrammed regulators that keep the body functioning as it should and react in a way that ensures survival. This brain reigned supreme in the reptilian age - imagine a snake hissing to signal the threat of an attack.

From the most primitive root, the brain stem, the emotional centers emerged. Millions of years later, in evolution, from these emotional areas evolved the thinking brain or "neocortex", the large bulb of twisted tissues that make up the upper layers. The fact that the thinking brain has grown from the emotional one reveals much about the relationship between thought and feeling; there was an emotional brain long before there was a rational one.

The oldest root of our emotional life is in the sense of smell, or, more precisely, in the olfactory lobe, the cells that absorb and analyze the sense of smell. Every living entity, be it nourishing, poisonous, sexual partner, predator or prey, has a distinctive molecular signature that can be carried by the wind. In those primitive times, the smell was proposed as a fundamental sense for survival.

From the olfactory lobe the ancient emotion centers began to evolve, eventually becoming enlarged enough to surround the upper part of the brain stem. In its rudimentary phases, the olfactory center was composed of little more than thin layers of neurons collected to analyze the sense of smell. A layer of cells absorbed the odor and divided it into relevant categories: edible or toxic, sexually available, enemy or meal. A second layer of cells sent reflective messages throughout the nervous system telling the body what to do: bite, spit, approach, run, chase.

With the arrival of the first mammals, new key layers of the emotional brain arrived. These, which surround the brain stem, roughly resemble a bagel with a bite taken out at the bottom where the brain stem nestles in them. Since this part of the brain surrounds and borders the brain stem, it has been called the "limbic" system, from "limbus", the Latin word for "ring". This new neural territory added emotions of the brain's repertoire. When we are in the throes of greed or fury, madly in love or retreating in fear, it is the limbic system that holds us in its grip.

As the limbic system has evolved, it has perfected two powerful tools: learning and memory. These revolutionary advances have allowed an animal to be much more intelligent in its survival choices and to fine-tune its responses by adapting to changing demands rather than having invariable and automatic reactions. If a food causes disease, it could be avoided next time. Decisions such as knowing what to eat and what to refuse were still largely determined by smell; the connections between the olfactory bulb and the limbic system now took on the task of making distinctions between smells and recognizing them, comparing a presents cent with past ones, and thus distinguishing good from bad. This was done by the "rhinencephalon", literally, the "brain of the nose", a part of the limbic wiring and the rudimentary base of the neocortex, the thinking brain.

About 100 million years ago, the mammalian brain underwent strong growth. Stacked on top of the thin two-layered cortex - regions that plan, understand what is perceived, coordinate movement - several new layers of brain cells have been added to form the neocortex. In contrast to the two-layered cortex of the ancient brain, the neocortex offered an extraordinary intellectual advantage.

The neocortex of Homo sapiens, much larger than in any other species, has added everything that is distinctly human. The neocortex is the seat of thought; it contains the centers that bring together and understand what the senses perceive. It adds to a sensation what we think about it and allows us to have feelings about ideas, art, symbols, imaginations.

In evolution, the neocortex has allowed for a judicious tuning that no doubt has enormously benefited an organism's ability to survive adversity, making it more likely that its progeny will in turn transmit genes that contain the same neural circuitry. The survival advantage is due to the neocortex's talent for strategy, long-term planning, and other mental tricks. Beyond that, the triumphs of art, civilization and culture are all fruits of the neocortex.

This new addition to the brain allowed for the addition of nuances to the emotional life; getting love. Limbic structures generate feelings of pleasure and sexual desire, the emotions that fuel sexual passion. But the addition of the neocortex and its connections to the limbic system has allowed the mother-child bond that underlies family unity and the long-term commitment to the infant dream that makes human development possible. (Species that have no neocortex, such as reptiles, lack maternal affection; when their young hatch, babies must hide to avoid being cannibalized). In humans, the protective bond between parent and child allows much of the maturation continues throughout a long childhood, during which the brain continues to develop.

As we move up the phylogenetic scale from reptilian to rhesus to human, the pure mass of the neocortex increases; with that increase comes a geometric increase in the interconnections in the brain circuits. The greater the number of such connections, the greater the range of possible responses. The neocortex allows for subtlety and complexity of emotional life, such as the ability to have feelings about our feelings. There is more neocortex to limbic system in primates than in other species - and much more in humans - suggesting why we are able to show a much wider range of reactions to our emotions and more nuances. While a rabbit or rhesus has a limited set of typical fear responses, the larger human neocortex allows for a much more agile repertoire, including calling the emergency telephone number.

But these higher centers do not govern all emotional life; in crucial matters of the heart - and especially in emotional emergencies - they can be said to refer to the limbic system. Since many of the higher centers of the brain have been born or extended into the limbic area, the emotional brain plays a crucial role in neural architecture. Like the root from which the newest brain grew, emotional areas intertwine through a myriad of connecting circuits to all parts of the neocortex. This gives the emotional centers immense power to influence the functioning of the rest of the brain, including its thought centers.

Emotions vs Brain

The connections between the amygdala (and its limbic structures) and the neocortex are the focus of the battles or cooperation treaties concluded between head and heart, thought and feeling. This circuit explains why emotion is so crucial to effective thinking, both for making wise decisions and simply for allowing us to think clearly.

Take the power of emotions to stop thinking itself. Neuroscientists use the term "working memory" for the attention span that keeps in mind the essential facts to complete a given task or problem, whether it is the ideal characteristics people look for in a home while visiting different elevations, or of the elements of a reasoning problem on a test. The prefrontal cortex is the brain region responsible for working memory. But the circuits from the limbic brain to the prefrontal lobes mean that the signals of strong emotions - anxiety, anger and suchlike - can create neural static, sabotaging the prefrontal lobe's ability to maintain working memory. This is why when we are emotionally upset we say that "we simply cannot think clearly" and why ongoing emotional distress can create deficits in a child's intellectual abilities.

These deficits, although more subtle, are not always exploited by IQ tests, although they manifest themselves through more targeted neuropsychological measures, as well as in a child's continued agitation and impulsiveness. In a study, for example, primary school children who had above average IQ scores but still did poorly at school found impaired frontal cortex functioning through these neuropsychological tests. They were also impulsive and anxious, often disturbing and in trouble, suggesting faulty prefrontal control over their limbic impulses. Despite their intellectual potential, these are the children at the highest risk of problems like school failure, alcoholism and crime, not because their intellect is deficient, but because their control over their emotional life is compromised. The emotional brain, quite separate from those cortical areas exploited by IQ tests, controls anger and compassion alike. These emotional circuits are sculpted by experience in childhood and we leave those experiences completely to chance at our peril.

Also consider the role of emotions in even the most "rational" decision-making process. In work with far-reaching implications for understanding mental life, leading researchers have conducted careful studies of what is impaired in patients with prefrontal amygdala damage. Their decision making is terribly flawed, yet they show no deterioration in IQ or any cognitive ability. Despite their intact intelligence, they make disastrous choices in business and in their personal lives, and can even obsess over and over about a decision as simple as when to make an appointment.

Leading researchers argue that their decisions are so bad because they have lost access to their emotional learning. As a meeting point between thought and emotion, the prefrontal-amygdala circuit is a crucial gateway for the deposit of likes and dislikes that we acquire throughout life. Cut off from emotional memory in the amygdala, whatever the neocortex mulls over no longer triggers the emotional reactions that have been associated with it in the past: everything takes on a gray neutrality. A stimulus, be it a favorite pet or a hated acquaintance, no longer triggers either attraction or aversion; these patients have "forgotten" all these emotional lessons because they no longer have access to where they are stored in the amygdala.

Evidence such as this leads to the counter-intuitive position that feelings are typically indispensable for rational decisions; they point us in the right direction, where dry logic can therefore be of better use. While the world often confronts us with a cumbersome array of choices (how should you invest your retirement savings? Who should you marry?), the emotional learning that life has given us (such as the memory of a disastrous investment or a painful breakup) sends signals that streamline the decision by eliminating some options and highlighting others early on. In this way, the emotional brain is as involved in reasoning as is the thinking brain.

Emotions, therefore, count for rationality. In the dance of feeling and thinking, the emotional faculty guides our decisions from moment to moment, working side by side with the rational mind, enabling - or disabling - thought itself. Similarly, the thinking brain plays an executive role in our emotions, except in those moments when emotions rise out of control and the emotional brain is rampant.

In a sense we have two brains, two minds and two different types of intelligence: rational and emotional. How we live is determined by both: it is not just IQ, but emotional intelligence that matters. In fact, intellect cannot function at its best without emotional intelligence. Normally the complementarity of the limbic system and the neocortex, the amygdala and the prefrontal lobes, means that everyone is a full partner in mental life. When these partners interact well, emotional intelligence increases, as does intellectual ability.

This overturns the old understanding of the tension between reason and feeling: it's not that we want to do away with emotion and put reason back in its place, as Erasmus did, but instead find the intelligent balance of the two. The old paradigm contained an ideal of reason freed from the attraction of emotion. The new paradigm pushes us to harmonize head and heart. Doing this well in our life means that we must first understand more exactly what it means to use emotions intelligently.

CHAPTER 3

IMPROVE EMOTIONAL INTELLIGENCE

Get in Touch With Your Emotions

Observe your emotional reactions to the events of daily life. It is easy to put aside the feelings related to what you experience in the space of a day. However, to improve your emotional intelligence, it is essential to take the time to recognize the emotions that have arisen from various experiences. If you ignore what you are feeling, you also overlook important information that profoundly affects your mental disposition and behavior. Then, start paying more attention to what you feel and connect those feelings to what you are experiencing.

For example, let's say you are completely ignored during a meeting. What emotions would arise in such a situation? Instead, how would you feel if your hard work was clearly appreciated? As you get used to naming a variety of feelings, including sadness, embarrassment, joy, and satisfaction, you will increase your emotional intelligence.

Get in the habit of getting in touch with your emotions at certain times of the day. What are the first sensations you feel when you wake up? And what are the ones you feel before falling asleep?

Pay attention to your body. Instead of ignoring the way your emotions manifest on the physical plane, start listening to them. Mind and body are not two separate entities, but they can influence each other quite deeply. You can improve your emotional intelligence by learning to interpret physical cues that help you understand what you are feeling. For example:

- stress can cause you to feel a kind of knot in the stomach, accompanied by pressure in the chest and rapid breathing;
- sadness could foster a sense of slowness and heaviness in the limbs;
- joy, pleasure, and nervousness can make you feel butterflies in your stomach, cause your heart to beat wildly and give you a boost of energy.

Notice how feelings and behaviors relate to each other. When you feel strong emotion, how do you react? Try to sense your gut reactions to everyday situations instead of reacting without thinking. The more you know the stimuli behind your behaviors, the more you will increase your emotional intelligence and will be able to use what you learn to correct yourself in the future. Here are some behaviors and what they actually hide:

- embarrassment and insecurity can take you away from a conversation and prevent you from taking part in it;
- anger can cause you to raise your voice or walk away in a rage;

- the feeling of oppression can make you panic, lose sight of what you were doing, and even cry.

Avoid judging your emotions. They are all legitimate, even the negative ones. If you judge them, you will prevent yourself from fully perceiving them and, therefore, it will be more difficult to put them to use. Let's put it this way: every emotion you experience encapsulates new, useful information and connects to the reality you are experiencing. Without this information, you wouldn't know how to react properly. This is why the ability to feel one people's emotions is a form of intelligence.

It's hard at first, but get used to bringing out negative feelings and connecting them to what's happening to you. For example, if you are a very envious person, what clues does this feeling offer you in relation to what you are experiencing?

Live even the most pleasant feelings to the full. Connect the joy and satisfaction to your surroundings so that you learn to hear them more often.

Observe the emotional patterns that repeat themselves. It's another way to deepen your feelings and how they relate to what you are experiencing. When you feel a strong emotion, ask yourself when was the last time you felt this way. What happened before, during and after?

If you are able to notice repeating patterns, you have the ability to exert more control over your behaviors. Look at how you handled a certain situation and ask yourself how you would like to deal with it in the future.

Keep a journal to describe your emotional reactions or moods from day to day. This way, you can clearly see how you tend to react.

Learn to behave. You cannot control the emotions you feel, but you can keep in touch with what happens in reality. It is worth reiterating that, without the information dictated by the circumstances, you would not know how to react adequately.

Learn to react. You can't control the emotions you feel, but you can decide how to react when they emerge. If you tend to verbally attack or withdraw into yourself every time you feel offended, think about the reaction you would like to adopt. Don't let emotions take over, but decide how you should behave when they try to overwhelm you.

When you go through an unpleasant time, try to feel your mood. Some describe this moment as a suffocating wave of sadness or anger. Once it's over, decide how you want to behave. Make an effort to communicate what you are feeling rather than repressing it, or stand up and take another attempt instead of throwing in the towel.

Don't get used to running away from situations. It is not easy to let negative feelings emerge, indeed many people repress them by throwing themselves into alcohol, spending whole days in front of the television or taking refuge in other vices that anesthetize them from pain. If this happens to you too often, there is a risk that your emotional intelligence will start to suffer.

Get in Touch With Other People

Try to broaden your mind and be friendly. Open-mindedness and friendliness go hand in hand when it comes to emotional intelligence. Typically, a narrow mindset indicates poor EQ. However, if you are open to understanding and introspective reflection, you can deal with disagreements with calm and self-confidence. You will gain a greater awareness of relationships with others and you will have new possibilities. Here are some elements that allow you to improve your emotional intelligence:

o listen to TV or radio debates. Consider the arguments of both sides and take note of the details that require deeper analysis. When someone exhibits a different emotional reaction than you would if you were in the same situation, consider the reason and try to see things from their point of view;

o improve your empathic skills. Empathy means being able to put yourself in the shoes of others by perceiving their emotions in this way. By actively listening and paying attention to what people are saying, you can get a better idea of their feelings. If you can use this information to make wise decisions and improve your relationships, you will demonstrate that you are emotionally intelligent;

o to improve your empathic skills, put yourself in others' shoes. Think about how you would feel if you were in the same situation as them. Imagine what it means to live their experiences and what support you would offer to alleviate their difficulties;

o when someone feels strong emotion, ask yourself, "How would I react in his place?" When someone confides in you, pay attention to what they say so you can treat them gently. Instead of mind wandering, ask questions and summarize what they are telling you so they understand that you are involved in the conversation.

o study body language. Make an effort to read between the lines and grasp people's true feelings by observing their facial expressions and gestures. Often, people say one thing, while their eyes reveal a deeper truth. Practice observing carefully and guessing the less obvious ways in which people communicate their emotions;

o if you can't interpret facial expressions, try taking a questionnaire to find out what you can improve on. The tone of the voice can reveal many other things. For example, if it's high, it indicates stress;

o observe the effect you have on others. Understanding the emotions of others is just one more step that allows you to improve your emotional intelligence. You also need to understand what effect you have on people. Do you tend to make them nervous, feel better or angry? How does a conversation change when you walk into a room?;

o think about the patterns you should change. If you tend to argue with people who love you, if your girlfriend has an easy crying when you talk, or if people don't unbutton too much when you're around, maybe you need to change your attitude in order to have a better effect on people.

o ask close friends or your partner if they think you are sensitive and if there is room for improvement. The tone of the voice also has its importance. You may have a hard time recognizing the effect you have on others, but those who know you can help;

o get used to being emotionally honest. If you say you are "fine" but have a grim expression, you are not sincere. Learn to clearly express your emotions with your body as well so that people can understand you better. Tell others that you are in a bad mood when you are angry, but also try to express joy and happiness in the best moments. If you are what you are, you will allow others to know and trust you because they will understand your intentions.

However, remember that there is a limit to be respected: control your emotions by avoiding hurting others.

Employing Emotional Intelligence

Find out what you can improve on. It is important in life to have good intellectual skills, but it is equally important to be emotionally intelligent. Having a great EI can foster relationships and professional opportunities. This ability consists of four fundamental elements that allow you to live in a balanced way. Read the following and try to understand where you can improve, then get to work.

Self-awareness: the ability to recognize people's emotions for what they are and understand where they come from. Self-awareness means knowing your strengths and limitations.

Self-management: the ability to postpone gratifications, balance people's needs with those of others, take initiative and moderate impulsiveness. It means knowing how to deal with changes and keep your word.

Awareness in the social sphere: the ability to perceive the emotions and concerns of others, but also to identify and adapt to the signals sent by the community. Acquiring awareness of social relationships means knowing how to notice the dynamics of power taking place within a group or an organizational context.

Relationship Management: the ability to get along with others, manage conflicts, inspire and influence people, and communicate clearly.

Beat stress by improving emotional intelligence. Stress is a generic word used to describe all the suffocating sensations due to various emotions. Life is full of difficult situations ranging from the end of romantic relationships to the loss of a job. In between, there are a myriad of factors that can further complicate everyday problems. If you are very stressed, you have a hard time behaving as you would like. A good plan to relieve tension allows you to improve your emotional intelligence in several ways.

Find out what triggers your stress and what helps you relieve it. List the most effective ways to reduce it (like hanging out with friends or taking a nature walk) and put them to good use.

Get help if needed. If stress is unbearable and you can't manage it, contact a psychologist or psychotherapist who can provide you with the right tools to deal with it (and also improve your emotional intelligence).

CHAPTER 4

16 PERSONALITY TYPES

Have you noticed what percentage personality quizzes there are on the Internet? DISC, Enneagram types, and therefore the Big 5 Personality types are just a few, and every one of them aim to offer the reader a far better understanding of their own personality type.

The most popular test in 2020 is the 16 personalities MBTI test, which stands for Myers-Briggs Type Indicator test. Like many of today's theories of personality typologies, it's supported by the work of Swiss psychologist and psychiatrist Jung, who wrote Psychological Types in 1921, and therefore the research of Isabel Briggs Myers and Katharine Cook Briggs. Jung was the founding father of analytical psychology, which studies the motivations underlying human behavior. The Jung personality types function an immediate foundation that made the Myers-Briggs 16 test possible.

Psychologists are debating for years over which the simplest personality types test is and which test gives the foremost accurate breakdown of the 16 personality types. The reality is, all of them can assist you gain more insights into different aspects of your personality.

Determining Personality Type

If you're taking the Myers-Briggs test, your personality typeis going to be an acronym made from four letters: ESTJ, ISTJ, ENTJ, INTJ, ESTP, ISTP, ENTP, INTP, ESFJ, ISFJ, ENFJ, INFJ, ESFP, ISFP, ENFP, or INFP.

What do represent the letters within the Myers-Briggs test? In accordance with Carl G. Jung's theory of psychological types, your personality type is decided by your preferences:

- introvert stands for "I";
- extravert stands for "E";
- thinking stands for "T";
- feeling stands for "F";
- sensing stands for "S";
- intuition stands for "I";
- judging stands for "J";
- perceiving stands for "P".

Combining the letters related to your dominant function leads you to your Myers Briggs personality type. If, for instance , your four preferences are Introverted (I), Sensing (S), Feeling (F) and Judging (J), your personality type is ISFJ. All possible combinations of the four preferences yield 16 different personality types.

The total of eight letters are grouped in 4 personality categories, as follows:

- introversion/extraversion: how you expend energy;
- sensing/intuition: how you receive information;
- thinking/feeling: how you create decisions;

-   judging/perceiving: how you see the planet.

No psychological type is best than another. All personality types have their strengths and weaknesses, and every person features a unique set of equally valuable characteristics. Understanding your distinctive personality archetypes are often useful in some ways, including relationships, career and learning.

The 16 Personality Types
The 16 personality types are grouped by 4 temperaments: Intellectuals, Visionaries, Protectors and Creators. Intellectuals are known for his or her rationality and intellectual superiority, Visionaries are known for his or her empathy and idealism, Protectors are known for his or her practicality and orderliness and Creators are known for his or her spontaneity and versatile nature.

The Four Temperaments

SJ – The "Protector"
Protectors (SJs) are dependable, altruistic and honest. They're driven by a strict work ethic and place a high premium on helping others and serving the community. Protectors are gifted leaders due to their aptitude to arrange, plan and strategize. They thrive in situations where they know what's expected. They appreciate rules and structure.

SP – The "Creator"
Creators (SPs) are naturally artistic, brave and adaptable. They appreciate the sweetness in nature, fashion and decoration. Their adventurous nature makes them excitable,

energetic and spontaneous. Driven by their curiosity and playfulness, Creators are willing to undertake almost anything. They're likable and popular. They like to tell an honest story.

NT – The "Intellectual"
Intellectuals (NTs) are intelligent, independent and determined. They're high-achievers, driven not only to accumulate but also to master large amounts of data. They're self-sufficient, logical and value reason. They seek to understand everything and can question anything. Their keen interest in investigation makes them great researchers and inventors.

NF – The "Visionary"
Visionaries (NFs) are empathetic, generous and original. They're caring individuals who aren't only sensitive to the emotions of others but also very adept at identifying them. They're idealistic and are driven by values they deeply believe and defend. Visionaries desire to know themselves and to be understood for who they really are.

16 Personalities Compatibility

Intellectual types
The Intellectual personality typesare characterized by: the Strategist, the Engineer, the Chief, and therefore the Originator. These MBTI types are introspective, logical, and continually seeking knowledge. Naturally curious and inventive, they hold a special love and devotion to

rationality. Despite their rational mindset and feet-on-the-ground approach, they're often very imaginative and are compelled to explore matters on a deeper level. This love for experiments and speculations makes these MBTI personalities a valuable asset in any community. Stupid questions don't exist to the Intellectuals — they're always able to brainstorm.

The Intellectual types correspond to the Choleric temperament from the 4 temperament types.

The Strategist (INTJ)

INTJs breeze through life with their undying belief within the strength of human knowledge and wit. They spend the bulk of their time analyzing situations to undertake to seek out ways to enhance on them. They're very disciplined and thrive on knowledge — being deemed "bookworms" in their early years is one among their main personality archetypes. However, there's no other label that the Strategist would relate to more. These people are unbothered by the overall opinion of the masses and aren't afraid to pursue their own philosophy of life. Avoiding the spotlight and dealing from the shadows, this sort is usually seen alone — but they don't mind this in the least. For them, every move they create in life is carefully considered and planned beforehand — life is sort of a giant chessboard for this Myers-Briggs personality type, and they are the grandmaster players that move the pieces.

Strategists are smart — and that they realize it. This however can cause others seeing them as arrogant, due to their high self-confidence and perception that they're intellectually superior to those around them. Other points within the INTJ's personality traits list are that they will be judgmental and take their tendency to be analytical a step too far. On the plus side — there's little to zilch they can't achieve. Valuing diligence, determination, and consistency, their mantra in life is that nothing is impossible if you're willing to pour the required energy and time into it.

The Engineer (INTP)
Brilliant theorists, guided by unquestionable logic and rationality, out of all the 16 personalities, INTP are the foremost logically precise. It's easy for them to identify problems and take into consideration all the factors that are involved when creating an answer. Typically reserved and even loners, Engineers pride themselves on their unique perspectives, intellect, and creativity. They're wont to people "not getting them" and if you're their friend, don't expect to seek out emotional support from their side once you need it. This personality sort of Myers-Briggs is more likely to supply you a series of well thought out suggestions on the way to affect your problem, instead of empathizing with it. This rational approach can often be met with disapproval from more sensitive types. Emotionality is confusing for Engineers — they simply don't find logic in it.
It's common for INTPs to possess trouble getting their messages across. It's not because they can't articulate them properly — others simply have trouble maintaining with their sharp minds. This will be very frustrating for people with these personality profiles, as they don't wish to hamper and simplify their notions for his or her listener's sake. The standard "never mind" with which they dismiss conversation once they finally hand over are often seen as condescending. However, once you are in need of an abstract thinker and solver — they're definitely your person.

The Chief (ENTJ)

ENTJs know a thing or two about leadership — and they aren't afraid to demonstrate it. They're people that live for accomplishment and spare no time when a choice has got to be made. These qualities, combined with their personality inventory of natural charisma and appeal, make them superb leaders. However, given their extreme determination and frequent "the end justifies the means" mindset, they'll seem ruthless and overwhelming to less strong characters. This is often why understanding these personality types could be a touch difficult.

Dominant, with little room for compromise, Chiefs enjoy an honest challenge and thrive at a chance to pour their energy in conquering it. They value people that are up to the task of matching their intellect and determination, and may be useful partners in achieving their goals. They know that regardless of how capable they are, they can't do everything alone, which is why ENTJs value the people around them.

A big a part of the personality profiling of ENTJs is their inflexibility to concentrate to other ideas than their own. This makes them very stubborn, especially when it involves suggestions supported emotional notions. They're also very impatient due to their quick-thinking and they have low tolerance for people that take too long to form a choice. While they will often come across as cold and insensitive, when it involves solving a crisis, they're the proper person to call. Very efficient, energetic and strong-willed, Chiefs often are a number of the foremost successful people around.

The Originator (ENTP)

No one likes intellectual sparring like the Originator. These people enjoy hearing different personality types' points of view and debating with them not due to any high stakes or higher purposes — often, it's simply entertaining. Like all Intellectual types, they're in constant pursuit of data, and acknowledge different perspectives from the MBTI grid as an honest thanks to broaden their own. They wish to challenge others and to question existing rules and regulations. This will make them invaluable in reworking systems, processes, and therefore the way things are done. Sometimes they will get trapped within the excitement of winning an argument to the extent that they will forget that diplomacy and adaptability are additionally required to realize peace. They have a tendency to forget that not everyone likes conflict and most of the people actually steer faraway from it.

Not likely to keep faraway from a risky situation, ENTPs are charismatic brainstormers who think quickly on their feet and luxuriate in training their brains. Like all intellectual sorts of personalities, they will be perceived as insensitive and intolerant — they simply believe an excessive amount in their own brainpower. Unlike the opposite Intellectuals, they aren't keen on practical matters or taking action on their plans — they like to make the blueprints, instead of work on turning them into reality. This doesn't mean they're lazy — they simply have trouble focusing for prolonged periods of your time. Some MBTI celebrities of this sort are Clemens, Hanks and Edison

Visionary types
The Visionary personality types contains the Mentor, the Confidant, the Advocate, and therefore the Dreamer. These sorts of personalities are introspective, intuitive, and highly idealistic. They're compassionate people that want to assist out others and make the planet a far better place. For them, kindness is vital and they will willingly cooperate, instead of

compete, just like the Intellectuals. Naturally empathetic, they like to surround themselves with emotions and like deep conversations to chitchat. Very optimistic, caring and type, they don't have a drag being hospitable the planet, but should take care who they're vulnerable ahead of, to avoid being hurt. The deep intuition of those test types acts as helpful guidance in distinguishing that.

The Visionary types correspond to the Melancholic temperament from the 4 temperament types.

The Confidant (INFJ)

There is a reason that this personality type is the rarest one among all — out of all the 16 personality percentages, INFJs structure just one5% of all people. They're gentle, idealistic and sensitive, but still capable of creating decisions and carrying on with their goals. They aren't static spectators — their belief that good and love will save the planet compels them to act. However, these good intentions aren't always working for his or her benefit. When Confidants get too entangled with saving the planet, they easily forget that they have savings too. They need to remember to look out for themselves as well and project warmth and kindness inwardly too. The people around them need to remember this as well, and allow INFJs to retreat inside from time to time.

While their passion and noble battle to try to do good are often admirable, the INFJ personality type is susceptible to easy burnout. They have to seek out ways to excuse steam and to manage their tendency for privacy. Very sensitive to criticism or someone questioning their ways, Confidants can react very harshly once they perceive that somebody is putting an enormous interrogation point on their beliefs. Still, they're very creative and have an almost unnatural ability to attach with others. Given their knack for speaking in human terms and helping others, it makes it easy for people to trust them.

The Dreamer (INFP)
Like true idealists, the INFP personality type is usually on the lookout for meaning in their lives. Strong believers in good, they're rarely discouraged and like to consider the glass as half full. For them, good is everywhere — even within the worst of individuals. Albeit it's hard to get, they're going to smile and do their best to assist erupt. Their calm and reserved exterior could also be misleading, as they're bursting with passion and strife from the inside. Dreamers aren't curious about the fabric goods that their deeds will provide them with. Rather, they're more entranced by their pure intentions and desire to try todo good. They are often satisfied with these qualities and the way they are guided by the principles.
Out of all the 16 personalities, INFPs can have problems with taking things too personally when faced with criticism (similarly to their close cousins, INFJs). They also tend to be private, which may make them difficult to urge to understand. However, if someone puts within the effort to try to do so, they're going to be greatly rewarded. Dreamers are excellent people to stay around — their optimism is contagious and they often radiate a way of peace and harmony. Passionate and determined, this gentle and constant personality type is prepared to fight for what they believe.

The Mentor (ENFJ)
Warm, passionate and charismatic, out of all 16 personalities, ENFJs are the leaders people flock to and

follow, without a reconsideration. They don't like leading for the only sake of boosting their egos and self-esteem, as they need many that last. Rather, they need a real interest in bettering the planet and its people, striving to enhance the community in any way they will. It's easy for them to speak on a good range of levels, given their excellent language skills, so it's not hard for them to seek out an audience. Next to being drawn to their silver tongued skills, people also like their honest and raw sincerity. When Mentors see potential in someone, they're going to do whatever is required to assist the person develop it.

This high degree of involvement in other people's lives are often a touch overwhelming sometimes for the Mentors. If they indulge others too much, at some point they will begin to overthink and see flaws in themselves that aren't there. If they fail to measure to their own set ideals, this will impact their self-esteem greatly and leave them feeling hopeless. However, their charismatic tolerance and genuine interest in people are bound to never leave them feeling lonely. People are drawn to passion and honesty, which is why ENFJs tend to be surrounded by loving friends and family, which help lift them up and keep them grounded.

The Advocate (ENFP)
True free spirits, nothing excites the ENFP personality type quite making meaningful connections with people. For them, deep conversations are a source of great pleasure, as they thrive on hearing different points of view and explaining their own. For ENFPs, everything in life is connected in a method or another, and trying to untangle these knots and add up of the connections is exhilarating. They don't work

well with bounds and limitations, and being expressive is what they shine at. Great company, both at parties and at the workplace, these warm and positive individuals are easy to identify during a crowd. Enthusiastic rays of sunshine, which brighten the times of everyone around, few personality types are as creative and charismatic because the Advocates.

Being expressive as they are, sometimes ENFPs can struggle with handling a practical approach to their endless stream of ideas. Nearly as good as they are with arising with creative solutions, their follow-up practices are terrible or non-existent. They lack the methodical approach required to hold on with turning their ideas into reality — something that Intellectuals are excellent at. Combined with their tendency to overthink and troubles focusing, they create very poor project planners. However, if you are in need of curious, enthusiastic and sometimes wacky creative machines, out of the 16 personalities, ENFPs are the simplest people for the task.

Protector types
The Protector personality types contains the Overseer, the Examiner, the Supporter and therefore the Defender. the kinds of personality traits they share are grounded, observant, and motivated to take care of security. They're also the foremost common personality types — Protectors structure around 50% of the entire population on earth. Very self-motivated, Protectors know who they are and feel comfortable in their own skin. While stubborn, the MBTI descriptions of those types paint them as people that steer them faraway from drama as simply as possible. The moving force in their lives is to point out their love by taking care of

their loved ones during a practical and subtle way. They have a tendency to figure hard and see things through — this is often provoked by their strong inner principles, like diligence and respect. Reliable, honest and industrious, they create excellent leaders.

The Protector types correspond to the Phlegmatic temperament from the 4 temperament types.

The Examiner (ISTJ)

Responsible, loyal and hard-working, Examiners value order and procedures. They need an acute sense of right and wrong and exerting in preserving established traditions and norms. While this might seem uptight to more fun-loving and free spirited personality types (like the Visionaries), ISTJs take particular pride in standing behind their actions. Not quick to assume, they like to carefully look around the cold facts before setting their mind on a choice. Their sharp fact-based minds make them the MBTI personality type that has the smallest amount tolerance for improbable theories or empty ramblings. With their blunt approach and unapologetic honesty, they could come off as cold and robotic, but within the head of the Examiner everything is usually justified and solidified by carefully analyzed factors. This stubbornness can cause them problems — Examiners don't wish to admit they were wrong during a situation. They can't come to terms with the notion that sometimes following rules "by the book" might not be so good and a more innovative approach is required. This, in turn, can cause them seeing as judgmental, as they need little regard for palaver. However, their honest bluntness also can be one among their biggest strengths, if used correctly. Their responsibility, strong will and practical nature makes them excellent workers in responsible positions.

The Defender (ISFJ)

Loyal and quiet traditionalists, ISFJs are true altruists, who give out the maximum amount kindness within the world as possible — sometimes eventoo much. Consistent with the MBTI test, they're responsible and you'll calculate them to urge the work done, albeit they have a tendency to procrastinate sometimes. Defenders wish to please others, so don't be surprised if they are going above and beyond to exceed the expectations that are assail them. Despite this quality, however, they don't enjoy taking credit for his or her accomplishments. This will make it easy for more selfish people to require advantage of them. Albeit they're introverted, Defenders have an unmatched ability to attach with people on a deeper emotional level and usually enjoy socialization.

The humble nature of the ISFJ are often their biggest challenge to face. They have to find out to face up for themselves an equivalent way they get up for people they look after. Their tendency for perfectionism also can cause them overloading themselves, both with workload and emotions. Despite that, they're extremely supportive, reliable and constant people to possess around, who enjoy giving attention to detail. You'll make certain that you simply can calculate them, as they're going to always have your back, regardless of what.

The Overseer (ESTJ)

According to the Myers-Briggs test, ESTJs are the personification of excellent old traditional values, like purposeful honesty, leading by example and doing everything with utmost dedication. They enjoy bringing communities together and leading them in preserving traditional celebrations. When working along side others, they expect them to act an equivalent way as an Overseer would — being competent, honest and hard working. If their expectations aren't met, an ESTJ can get angry very quickly. This solidifies their tendency to be inflexible (just like all Protector types), but this is often just because they believe that those mechanisms are essential to form the planet run smoothly. Overseers are truth model citizen — they rarely exit of place and do everything to stay up the great image of the community.

Their inflexibility can cause them issues where innovative solutions to problems are required. Because they trust data and facts so devotedly, they have a tendency to mistrust hunches and intuition, unless it's supported by concrete evidence. This also makes them bad at handling unorthodox situations, that a careful methodology isn't developed yet. However, they're excellent organizers, whose dedication is unmatched. The strong will of Overseers helps them perform this dedication, and their honest and reliable nature makes them invaluable in any community.

The Supporter (ESFJ)

ESFJs are very social and popular butterflies who value relationships and supporting and nurturing others. They wish to surround themselves with family and friends and always confirm that their loved ones are happy and okay. While they'll like gossip and discussing practicalities, those preferences don't stem from a nasty place. In particular else, out of all 16 personalities, ESFJs take their responsibility to assist others very seriously. They like to be of service and are up to doing almost anything to assist their community out, as long as they feel appreciated. You'll always calculate them to stay the harmony and stability in any group. Caring, thoughtful and warm, nothing can hurt Supporters quite someone rejecting their ideas or lacking interest in their activities.

Sometimes ESFJs can get trapped too in worry about their social station. Despite tons of their good qualities — loyal, dutiful, sensitive and warm — stemming from this preoccupation with status, it also can play them a nasty joke. It can cause them to be reluctant when it involves being flexible and improvising, and may make them especially susceptible to criticism. Their need for appreciation can sometimes be excessive for people of other personality types and may be suffocating. This is often why people of those Myers-Briggs personality traits got to remind themselves that always things aren't personally targeted towards them, but rather are a results of a special point of view.

Creator types

The Creator personality types contains the Persuader, the Craftsman, the Entertainer and therefore the Artist. These character personality types are self-reliant explorers, who don't mind leaving the trail without a map on a day-hike. Their impulsiveness teaches them to simply adapt to any situation. People with these personalities test low on being keen on obligations, and zip can frustrate them quite leading an uneventful life. This is often why they wish to spice things up for themselves and it's typical of them to always get on the move. Constantly on the lookout for brand spanking new experiences, it's never boring when a Creator is around.

The Creator types correspond to the Sanguine temperament from the 4 temperament types.

The Craftsman (ISTP)

These naturally curious handymen find it very difficult tokeep their hands still. The Myers-Briggs breakdown of Craftsmen is of individuals who wish to find out how things work — albeit it means disassembling them and putting them back together, just to review the intricate details that they're made from. They don't mind someone getting their hands dirty along side them, especially if it's a beloved. However, those people should confine mind that Craftsmen don't take lightly when someone interferes with their freedom and principles. This love of freedom can make it difficult for Craftsmen to respect the boundaries that others lay down for them. This causes them to sometimes act inappropriately, consistent with social norms — for instance they're the first to tell an insensitive joke.

ISTP stubbornness, difficulty to validate others' emotions and tendency to urge easily bored can all trigger them to interact in risky behavior. When combined with logic, this spontaneity are often one among their biggest strengths, allowing them to simply slot in any new situation. Although they are always on the move, they are able to prioritize and are not quick to release their energy onto the planet. This makes them one among the simplest Myers-Briggs types to handle a crisis — their love for daring adventures and eagerness to urge their hands dirty helps during this respect.

The Artist (ISFP)

No other MBTI character is as wanting to challenge traditional expectations quite the ISFP. What's more, they are doing so with their daring and artistic view of the planet, expressed in their design and aesthetics. They are doing not recoil from challenging and reinventing themselves if they see fit. This creates a way of spontaneity about them, which may surprise even their closest family and friends. Artists, as

Myers-Briggs explained, have a knack for gambling and risky behavior, but their connection to their environment and therefore the moment often allows them to try to do better than many others. They enjoy connecting with others and typically have the right compliment stored up which will melt any heart. They're sensitive to harsh criticism and it is often hard for them to exit of the instant long enough to let things calm down.

The MBTI results for ISFPs are plain — they dislike commitments, which may cause them some problems during the course of their lives. Whether it's finding a partner, progressing at work or making important long-term plans, they have to find out the way to strengthen their weaknesses and make them their ally. This will be avoided compromising their beloved freedom — if they manage to get the fragile balance. Fortunately because of their charm and skill to relate to others' emotions, they're going to never walk alone. The curious, passionate and imaginative Artists are people that definitely leave their mark on the planet — in a method or another.

The Persuader (ESTP)

The Myers Briggs explanation of Persuaders is best described as a magnet that draws people. Their energetic, witty and humorous personalities are widely appreciated by those around them. They live for laughing and entertaining big crowds and aren't very keen on talking about abstract ideas or participating in complicated discussions about global issues. Instead, they like to bein the present — to speak in an easily understandable language, that folks find easy to attach to. They often find it hard to face still and like to leap into action instead of strategizing beforehand. This will mean that they find it hard to thrive in very organized structures, like school, not because they're not smart but because they clash with their hands-on-learning mentality.

Nothing goes unnoticed by ESTPs — their Myers-Briggs assessment is the most perceptive out of all the kinds. Using their observations and powerful intuition, they don't recoil from calling out people whenever they see fit. One thing they should remind themselves of often, however, is that not everyone is as open as they are - some people don't see eye-to-eye on having their personal lives passed on. It's not that they are doing this with malicious intent — it's just their straight shooting and colorful personality that can't be leashed by social norms. Precisely their down-to-earth, energetic and charming attitude is the reason why numerous people flock to them and are interested in their friendly enthusiasm.

The Entertainer (ESFP)

The energy of ESFPs is usually contagious — in social settings they're going to be the first to interrupt into a song or dance. These people enjoy excitement, love new adventures and are extremely people-oriented. Nothing brings Entertainers more happiness than sharing joyous moments with their friends. Due to their highly social nature, they're especially lively once they are the middle of attention and hate being alone. Funnily enough, they're the sort that has the strongest aesthetics sense out of all the Myers-Briggs personalities. They will often be seen expressing that sense of favor in their clothing choices, home decor and overall environment.

Even though they'll seem self-centered initially glance, this is often not the case in the least for ESFPs. They're sensitive to others' emotions and are happy to assist, should someone come to them with a drag to unravel. One among the most challenges they struggle with is coming to terms with the duties and responsibilities that bring them back to reality. They're the foremost likely Myers Briggs test type to believe luck and the help of their friends, instead of doing the hard and sometimes boring work that precedes fun activities. They're often poor at planning, which may frustrate them when it involves reaching a much bigger, long-term goal. They have to acknowledge these weaknesses in their personality and actively work to beat them, otherwise they risk potential unhappiness.

16 Personalities Compatibility

When it involves finding your best match, the 16 personalities test is perhaps the simplest relationship test out there. If you're interested by which types go well together, take a glance at the MBTI compatibility chart listed below.

As well as getting used as something of a relationship guide, the MBTI personality type test can have more useful applications. On the one hand it is often used as a useful job test, with which employees are often better matched with jobs they will shine at.

Emotional Intelligence

Type:	Compatible with:		
ESFP	ESFJ	ESTP	ISFP
ESTP	ESTJ	ESFP	INFJ
ESTJ	ESTP	ESFJ	ISTJ
ESFJ	ISTP	ESTJ	ESTP
ISTJ	INFJ	ISTP	ISFJ
ISTP	ISFP	INFP	ESFP
ISFJ	ESFJ	ISFP	ISTJ
ISFP	ESFP	ISFJ	ESFJ
ENTJ	INTJ	ENTP	ENFJ
ENTP	ENTJ	ENFP	ENFJ
ENFJ	ENFJ	INFJ	ENFP
ENFP	ENTJ	INTJ	INTP
INTJ	INTP	INFJ	INFP
INTP	ENTP	INFP	ENFP
INFJ	ISTJ	INFP	INTJ
INFP	INFJ	ISFJ	ENFJ

CHAPTER 5

LEARN TO CONTROL YOUR EMOTIONS

Emotions can be uncomfortable and even scary at times. However, know that there is nothing inherently "wrong" about trying them, whatever they are. Controlling your feelings does not mean ignoring or repressing them, rather it means learning to process and react in a healthy and useful way. Think of this process as a way to "regulate" your emotions, just like you would a thermostat. By learning to control your feelings, as well as feeling more stable, you can also improve your physical condition!

Control Emotions in the Moment

Stop and take back control. It can be easy to get overwhelmed by an emotion and have unwanted reactions. If you start to notice that you are being drawn into a spiral of uncontrollable emotional reactions, take a step back from what is happening and focus on what you feel physically. In this way, by detaching yourself from the current situation, you have the possibility of "taking away" the mind from the sense of oppression.

When you are emotionally provoked, you will likely experience a range of physical sensations, such as increased heart rate, muscle tension, and rapid breathing or wheezing.

Most people develop emotional reactions which are grouped under the definition of "autonomic reactivity". It is a "mental habit" that forms as an automatic response of a certain type to stimuli that come from emotionally demanding situations. You may feel like you don't control such reactions; fortunately, you have the opportunity to rearrange your mind by focusing on the present.

Consciously examine your body's reactions. Imagine you are a doctor observing a patient. For example, if you suddenly feel anxious, notice what is happening in your body: rapid heartbeat, sweaty hands, nausea. Identify and accept these feelings as they are, rather than considering them "wrong" or trying to get rid of them.

Awareness is actually made up of many information paths that tell us something simultaneously. The sense of oppression can be caused by perceiving emotional reactions as a jumble of sensations and sensory experiences in a tangled way. Stop and try to focus on one thing at a time, such as smells, what you touch or what you see. This will help the brain learn to process these information pathways more effectively, without getting caught up in the whirlwind of emotions.

Take control of your breath. When the body experiences intense emotions, you may enter the physical "fight or flight" mode. This response activates the sympathetic nervous system which circulates adrenaline and other chemicals, which increase the heart rate, create breathlessness and cause muscle tension.

By breathing deeply and regularly, you can calm down and receive the oxygen your body needs to relax.

Place one hand on your chest and the other on your abdomen, under the rib cage. Inhale slowly and deeply through your nose, counting to 4. Try to feel your lungs and abdomen expand as you let the air in.

Hold your breath for 1 to 2 seconds, then slowly release it through your mouth. Aim to take 6-10 deep breaths per minute.

If you can't make it to 4, start counting to 2 and increase with practice. Just try to breathe as deeply and regularly as you can.

Try progressive muscle relaxation. It offers you the chance to calm down by systematically contracting and relaxing different muscle groups. This is a great way to relieve stress and tension. It can also help you recognize the signs of physical tension in your body.

If you can, allow yourself 15 minutes in a quiet and relaxing environment. However, if you can't find them, you can practice some progressive muscle relaxation techniques even while sitting at your desk.

Sit down and make yourself comfortable. Loosen tight clothing. Take deep, cleansing breaths.

You can start at the forehead and work your way down the body, or start at the toes and work your way up. In this example, we will start with the feet.

Start bending your toes as much as you can. Hold them in this position for 5 seconds, then relax. Enjoy the relaxing sensation for 15 seconds, then move on to the next muscle group.

Contract your calves, pulling your toes towards your face as hard as you can. Hold this position for 5 seconds, then relax. Again, relax for 15 seconds, then move on.

Continue to squeeze each muscle group for 5 seconds, then stretch out. Take a 15 second break between groups, paying attention to how you feel when you release the tension.

Proceed with each of the following groups: toes, feet, thighs, hips and buttocks, belly, back, shoulders, upper arms, forearms, hands, lips, eyes, forehead.

If you don't have enough time to contract and relax all muscle groups, focus on those in your face. By relaxing your facial muscles, you can relieve the feeling of stress. Studies have also shown that stretching your muscles and smiling can make you feel calmer and happier.

Use visualization techniques. Some people find imagining a relaxing experience to help control sudden emotional reactions. It will take time and practice, but once you can imagine your favorite context, you will have the ability to turn stressful moments into manageable situations.

Choose a "safe" place. It can be any place that you find peaceful and relaxing, such as a beach, spa, temple, or your bedroom. Just make sure it's a place where you feel safe and relaxed.

Close your eyes and imagine the "safe" place. Try to think about as many details as possible. What sounds do you hear? What do you see? What smells? What do you feel by the touch?

Breathe slowly and regularly. If you feel physical tension, use progressive muscle relaxation techniques or shake your muscles to loosen them.

You may feel uncomfortable or inexperienced the first few times you imagine your safe place. It is absolutely not a problem! Trust me, this exercise will work.

If you experience a negative emotion during the visualization process, try to think of it as a physical object that you can remove from the scenario. For example, you might imagine stress as a pebble to throw into the sea, away from the quiet beach you are on. As you throw the pebble, think that the stress is leaving your body.

Identify and Modify Useless Patterns With Which You Manage Emotions

Consider how emotions are handled in your family. Psychologists suggest that children acquire emotional regulation - the ability to govern and control their emotions by observing and emulating the patterns with which parents and family members deal with emotions. The way you learn to bond with your parents as a child can also affect the way you interact with others as an adult, in what is known as an "attachment style". Understanding how your emotions were handled when you were little can help you understand your current emotional habits. While it may be more helpful to review your experience with a mental health professional, there are some questions you may want to consider on your own:

- during your childhood, were conflicts faced openly or was there an "unwritten rule" that one should avoid talking about unpleasant things?
- how did your parents handle emotions? Did they show them or did they hide them? Did they explode or sulk?

- do you associate a particular emotion with a family member?
- what emotion do you struggle to bear? How does/ did your family manage it?
- were there emotions that were considered taboo in your family?

Consider what to do to resolve the situation. Sometimes, you may feel like you can't control your emotionality, because you can't see a way to resolve the situation that gives you certain emotions. In this case, you tend to "mull over" or follow the same thoughts as a "broken record", letting you obsess over negative considerations or feelings, usually with a vague and useless sense. Instead, try to focus on some specific elements of the situation that you may be facing.

For example, a rumination about work problems might look like this: "What's wrong with me? Why does it seem like things never get resolved? Why am I not good at anything in my job?" These vague and generic thoughts are unproductive and useless.

Instead, make a list of the things you can deal with. For example, you might talk to your boss about how to increase your performance, ask someone more experienced to guide you, educate you, or focus on stress management techniques that can make you feel more prepared to handle stress at work.

There are also aspects that, despite your best efforts, you will not be able to fix. It is important to accept this possibility. For example, if there is a co-worker who is spiteful and unpleasant at all, you cannot change his behavior. You have a chance to talk to him about how his attitude affects others, but you have to accept that it's up to him to put your words to good use or not. Giving up the idea of having to "fix" or "control" every element of a situation can be very liberating.

Learn to recognize and question cognitive distortions. Many of us have heard the expression "looking at the world with rose-colored glasses". Cognitive distortions are useless thought patterns, which encourage looking at the world through a filter that alters understanding.

Cognitive distortions come from allowing our emotions to convince us that something is true, without examining it. Fortunately, these are learned habits that can be broken with a little practice.

Recognize and counter the negative ideas that come from the feeling of inadequacy. Often the inadequacy stems from low self-esteem, the idea of not being good enough at something or not deserving someone. By identifying these distortions and challenging them when they arise, you will be able to train your mind to reject the "automatic" assumption of not being "good enough". The most common sprains include thinking that everything is black or white. Everything is good or bad, with no nuance between the extremes. If you are not perfect, then you are a failure. You can counter this thinking by showing compassion towards yourself and recognizing that everyone in the world faces challenges and sometimes makes mistakes. For example: "I ate that piece of cake for lunch, even though I'm trying to eat a healthier diet. I wish I hadn't, but it's not the end of the world. I can choose a healthier dinner."

Discredit the positives. The fact that someone speaks well of you doesn't matter. On the other hand, if someone talks badly about you, you just say "I always knew". Face this thought by looking for evidence of everything you do correctly in your life. You will find it, if you look closely.

Customize. You believe you are the cause of some negative event, when in reality you are not at fault. You center everything "on you": for example, "My wife looked really pissed when we talked on the phone before her. She is probably mad at me." Counter this belief by reflecting on other possible causes of events or situations that don't necessarily revolve around you: "My wife seemed really upset. Maybe she's having a hard day. Maybe she's not feeling well. I'll ask her how she is when we meet later".

Reading minds. You believe you know what others think or feel (usually, it's something negative) without asking them any questions. In particular, it feels like you know how people feel about you and how this affects their actions. For example, you think someone disrespects you and you don't bother to point it out; just assume it is. You do it because you feel you don't deserve respect and, therefore, you are particularly sensitive towards those who, in your opinion, could not respect you. Address this thought by asking others directly what they think and feel without formulating any prejudice.

Recognize and counter negative ideas that come from fear. We can fear many things. We let fear take over rationality because we are convinced that something bad is about to happen, even though we have no proof that it will. Once you understand that fear is at the root of these distortions, you can face them by stopping their spiral and seeking rational solutions.

Generalizing to the extreme. A single negative event turns into an endless pattern of defeats. "I haven't received a call. Nobody will look for me again" or "he/she left me. Why would anyone else want to go out with me?" You generalize not because of a pattern, but because you are afraid that the same pattern will repeat itself. Challenge it by remembering that this is a single event: examine the situation to see if there is actual evidence of an event paradigm. Did you go a couple of days without receiving a phone call? Is it possible that no one wanted to talk to you or that people have just been very busy?

Labeling and stigmatizing. This is an extreme form of generalization. When you make a mistake, you define yourself in a certain way, such as "I'm a loser". When you don't like someone's behavior, you are ready to give them a negative label, such as "they are a despicable person." Stigmatization involves a description of events in very colorful and emotionally charged language. As all-encompassing, it constitutes a problem. Counter this way of thinking by separating your actions or feelings from the truest part of you: "I feel bad because I didn't pass the exam. However, that doesn't make me a 'failure.' I'm good at many other things".

Jumping to conclusions. You interpret the facts negatively even when there is no evidence to support your thesis. You think being prepared for the worst, rather than hoping for the best, is the right thing to do, you are scared and hopeless. For example, you might assume that it is useless to propose an idea at a business meeting, because "it will definitely be rejected." Counter this way of thinking by stopping at each step and examining the validity of your conclusions.

Recognize and challenge negative ideas that come from other complex emotions. This kind of distortion can cause pain and guilt. When you find yourself thinking this way, stop for a moment. Look for rational evidence to support each assumption.

Emphasize (be catastrophic) or minimize. Imagine looking at yourself, or looking at someone else, through binoculars. You may believe that your mistake, or someone else's success, is more important than it really is. Now imagine you flip the binoculars, looking through the opposite side. Your action may appear less serious than it really is, as well as the responsibilities of others. This is how emphasis and minimization work. Combat such an attitude by having compassion for yourself and examining the evidence on which your considerations are based. For example, it is likely that for a graduate student the publication of his thesis is not something extraordinary because he believes that anyone can get it. You might question this minimization, remembering that most people don't publish their thesis at all, and that it's something to be proud of.

Reasoning by letting yourself be carried away by emotionality. You assume that your negative emotions necessarily reflect things as they are in reality: "I feel it, so it has to be true." You want the world to really be as you perceive it because it helps you feel less helpless. Challenge this kind of thinking by looking for the logic behind these conjectures. You can also remind yourself that your emotions are not facts.

Follow dictates with moral obligations. You force yourself to stay motivated to accomplish something. You should do this, you feel compelled to do that and so on. This way you will be led to act only because you feel guilty and not because you really want to. When you address your statements to others, you feel anger, frustration, and resentment. Counter these thoughts by replacing moral obligation with less heavy language: for example, "Today I should have gone running" could become: "It would have been a healthy choice to go running today".

Reacting to Unpleasant Emotions

Write down the evidence that supports or contradicts the thought that arose from a certain emotion. Start connecting the dots to better understand your reaction.
Thinking about it, you may realize that while no one particularly likes your boss, they just can't afford to fire anyone due to a lack of staff in your department.
For example, you may have said something that made him angry but now you have more time to retract. His reaction during lunch may not match what you initially thought.

Ask yourself: "Is there another way to look at the situation with more rationality and balance than I have done so far?". Evaluate every possibility. If nothing else, thinking of other possible interpretations will make you aware of the many possible scenarios and the futility of drawing hasty conclusions.

In light of the new considerations, you may conclude that despite the boss's annoying behavior, your job is safe, thereby alleviating the distress that was overwhelming you. If this method doesn't work, continue with the next step.

Consider your options. Now that you know the emotions to deal with, think about at least two possible ways to react. When you believe there is only one possibility, you are at the mercy of your emotions. However, you always have a second choice. For example, when someone insults you by making you angry, your instincts may advise you to react by returning the insult. However, no matter what emotion it is, there are always at least two alternatives, and you can probably imagine others as well, for example: doing nothing. This attitude is particularly effective when you know that a person is trying to annoy you with the sole purpose of disheartening you. If you stay calm, the person who is irritating you will become discouraged and eventually stop doing it.

Take it easy. Easy to say, hard to do, but there is some way to relax that doesn't require a lot of training, experience or willpower. When we are angry or upset, we tend to stiffen and agitate. Breathing deeply is a simple and effective way to relieve agitation. While it won't be able to completely dispel your anger, it can help you lessen it just enough so you don't want to say or do something you may later regret.
Do the opposite of what you would normally do. For example, when your partner refuses to wash the dishes, you can't help but get annoyed. Instead of starting a heated argument, calmly wash the dishes and tell your partner - in a calm, calm tone - that you would appreciate his help considering you do all the housework.

Get out of the situation. For example, if you are working on a project with a group of people who are not very focused, irritable and unproductive, you will most likely be in a bad mood during meetings. One of the possible strategies to overcome the agitation, frustration and anger is to get assigned to a different project. In practice, you will get out of a situation that would generate negative and useless feelings.

Make a choice. When deciding what to do, it is important to ensure that your choice is conscious and does not depend on emotionality. For example, if a person insults you and you decide not to react, do you do it because you have considered this solution in a rational way or because you fear confrontation? Here are some good reasons to take action:

- principles: what kind of person do you want to be? What are your moral principles? What result do you want to achieve from this situation? Basically, which decision would you be most proud of?
- logic: what kind of actions could reasonably lead you to the result you want?

Communicate assertively. Learning to communicate assertively can be very useful when you need to control your emotions, because it can help you express yourself in an open and healthy way. Being assertive doesn't mean hurting others' susceptibility or being arrogant. It means recognizing and respecting one's own needs and feelings, as well as those of others. Some ways to communicate assertively include:
Use first-person sentences. This type of communication can help you express your feelings without giving the impression that you are accusing or belittling those in front of you. For

example, if someone hurt your feelings, instead of saying, "You don't care about me," you might reply, "I was hurt seeing you didn't call me back when you said you would. What happened?".

Invite others to share their experiences. No circumstance has a single version of the facts. Invite others to share their thoughts and experiences with you, just like you do with them. You will get a clearer idea of what is going on and also show the people in front of you that you care about dialogue with them, rather than exploding into a monologue. For example, once you have expressed your opinion, you could go on asking, "What are your thoughts on this?".

Avoid "shoulds" and "musts". These statements, known as "categorical imperatives," can generate frustration and anger. They often blame or judge, either others or themselves. For example, instead of thinking, "My partner should never hurt my feelings," try remembering that we are all human and that we make mistakes every now and then. This way, you will be able not to get angry when you make mistakes, because you will be less inclined to take the situation personally.

Express your feelings clearly and directly. To communicate assertively, it is important not to "beat around the bush". It's not a problem if you reject requests that put you in awkward positions or you don't have time for. Just say what you think gracefully, but clearly. For example, if a friend invites you to a huge barbecue that you don't want to attend, you might say, "Thanks for thinking of me! Actually, I don't like being in crowded places, so I'd rather stay at home. How about meet for a coffee next week instead? ".

Reflect on Your Feelings

Identify how you feel. Sometimes, you may feel like you don't even know what you are feeling. If you take the time to reflect and isolate your feelings, you can structure your emotions, but you will also feel more stable and able to manage them. Understanding one's emotional universe on a regular basis increases self-awareness, which is a key component of self-confidence. Perhaps you can understand how you feel at a certain moment if you have a list of definitions handy to identify any emotions.

Make sure the list includes pleasant emotions, such as love, joy, wonder, understanding, fun, and hope.
Unpleasant emotions can include disgust, irritation, sadness, grief, anger, frustration, or sadness.
Remember that just because an emotion is unpleasant doesn't mean it's bad. Fear and anger, for example, have evolved to keep us safe from harm. They can alert us when there is a threat. The secret is knowing how to recognize when these feelings are not useful.
A list of "clues" can also help you identify what you are feeling. For example, a list of physical and behavioral clues about love might include: feeling excited, loving, or confident; rapid heartbeat; desire to hug or cuddle; need to say or be told "I love you".

Learn to distinguish primary and secondary emotions. Once you have identified the general feeling you are experiencing, it would be helpful to unravel the tangle of other emotions involved in your emotional experience. Feeling at the mercy of emotions means perceiving many sensations at once (or in rapid succession). Find a moment to reflect on each one.

For example, if your partner is chatting with another person at a party and you feel anger, this could be a primary emotion.

However, if you analyze what you think and feel, you may also find yourself jealous. Jealousy is actually a manifestation of fear: fear of not being "worthy" of someone else or of being abandoned, because you can only perceive what you see as negative, not the aspects that make you lovable.

You may find that you are actually angry with yourself, because the most critical part of you believes that you are stupid to think that your partner can love you by accepting all the sides of you that you don't like.

You may also feel embarrassed that your partner is paying attention to another person, instead of you. You may believe that others judge your relationship based on this.

Once you understand what other emotions come into play in a given situation, you will have a better understanding of the reason for your mood. You can also act so that you don't get overwhelmed by emotion.

For example, consider whether your reactions have a rational basis. If your partner has cheated on you in the past, you will probably feel more justified in becoming suspicious even when he interacts with other people in seemingly innocent ways. If your relationship is generally stable and happy, you might want to keep in mind that he has chosen to be with you and no one else.

Keep a diary. Writing down your emotions can teach you to identify what you are feeling. It is also useful for learning to recognize what can trigger certain emotions and the useful and useless ways to deal with them.

This exercise can also help you acknowledge an emotion as it appears, rather than giving it room to grow and intensify. If you ignore or repress your feelings, they will tend to get worse and explode later.

To keep a journal, just write down any moods or feelings you are experiencing and then reflect back from that moment, focusing on what may have aroused it. For example, your boss doesn't even glance at you at lunch. Without even realizing it, you may be thinking in the innermost part of your mind: "He's getting ready to fire me!" You become anxious or irritable for the rest of the day.

Ask yourself a few questions about what you wrote in your journal. Some may be: how do I feel right now? Do I think something has happened that caused this reaction? What do I need when I feel this way? Have I ever felt this way in the past?

As you update your diary, you should also accept your persona. Try not to judge your emotions, even those that you think are negative. Remember that you cannot control what you feel, but how you interpret and react to it.

Write about any events or experiences that leave a bad taste in your mouth. For example, maybe you yelled at a waiter because he spilled what you were drinking on you. Try writing what happened without judging anyone, not even yourself: "The waiter spilled coffee on me. I got mad and yelled at him. I was angry because I was wearing a new shirt that I really liked."

Remember that anyone can make mistakes. It's not an excuse for bad behavior, but a way of reminding yourself that you are a human being and, like all people, you do things you regret. By blaming yourself for something, you risk staying focused on the past rather than looking to the future.

Be kind to yourself. Forgive yourself when you are wrong. Think about how you can fix the situation. Think about how you intend to react in the future when similar circumstances arise and make a plan. For example: "I scolded that waiter and I don't like this behavior because I don't want to be rude to anyone. I allowed my anger to take over. If another incident happens, I'll have to remind myself that everyone, including me and everyone in front of me, makes mistakes. I'll speak kindly instead of getting angry".

Take responsibility for what you feel. When you try to blame other people for what you are feeling, admit it. This way you will be able to better control your emotions.

Consider your perspective. Studies have shown that people who are optimistic generally react better to stress. Learning to have a more positive outlook takes time and practice, but it can also improve your resilience to troubling or disturbing emotions and experiences.

Look for the positive aspects. People have a bad tendency to focus primarily on the negative sides of a certain situation, while neglecting the positives altogether. Take the time to list the nice little things that happen to you every day.

Learn to replace generic and permanent sentences with more accommodating and circumscribed ones. For example, you might be stressed about passing an important exam, thinking, "It's useless. I've been a sucker in history. Why do I have to be bored studying when I already know it will be a total failure?". This thinking assumes that your history skills are permanent, rather than something to be built through practice and commitment. This kind of attitude could make what you think come true, where failure stems from lack of dedication (due to the fact that you expect failure).

Alternatively, you might stress out an important exam first and think, "I'm afraid I'm not prepared enough. I'll use my time to work out other patterns and join a study group. I won't pass the exam with an excellent grade, but I will know that I did my best". By seeing the experience in the most flexible way - as something you can tweak with a little bit of effort - you'll have a better chance of success.

Challenge irrational preconceptions about yourself. There are many irrational ideas that repeatedly upset us. They are all false, but it happens that many of us are inclined to believe them real. Below, you will find some preconceptions about yourself that can keep you from feeling good about yourself.

"To be a person of value, I have to be perfect from every point of view." No one can be perfect in everything he does in his life. There is no standard of perfection, and if you rigidly follow an unattainable pattern, you will be destined to live a life filled with unhappiness. Instead, aim for an ideal that is important to you, but keep in mind that there is a reason why it is called an "ideal".

"I have to be loved and approved by whoever is important to me". Each person is unique, and some just don't mix well.

Trying to control others' reactions to what you do is not only useless, it will make you unhappy and dissatisfied.

"People who treat me badly are bad." Everyone makes mistakes. Most of the time, people don't even realize they are treating you badly. No one is infallible, nor always "good" or always "bad".

"It is unbearable to feel frustrated, abused or rejected." Some people are unable to bear even minimal levels of frustration. As a result, they continually lose their jobs and endanger their friendships because they are able to endure the slightest frustration. Be respectful towards others.

"I have to worry about anything that's dangerous or scary". Many people believe that "worrying" helps solve problems. They go to great lengths to search for something to worry about. "Ok that's it. What's next on the list I need to worry about?" Remember that you cannot control anything other than the way you act and react.

"It's terrible when things don't go exactly the way I want them to". Do you think you can predict the entire course of your life? Probably not. For the same reason, you cannot predict that things will go exactly the way you want - not even immediately.

Challenge negative beliefs about you. Your mindset may have developed certain beliefs about you so deeply that they are rooted. If you learn to recognize the prejudices you have developed about yourself, you will be able to overcome them.

"Unhappiness is due to external forces that I cannot control." Many inmates describe their life as if it were a cork, which rises and falls in the wake of circumstances. You can choose to see yourself as the cause or effect of situations. Take responsibility for your actions.

"Avoiding life's difficulties and responsibilities is easier than facing them". Even painful experiences, once overcome, can form a basis on which to learn and grow.

"Since things have controlled my life in the past, they will continue to do so in the present and in the future." If this were true, we would be prisoners of our past and changes would be impossible. However, people change all the time and sometimes radically! You have the ability to be whoever you want, you just have to believe in yourself.

"I can also be happy by doing nothing and taking life as it comes". If this were true, every wealthy person or person receiving a rich pension would do as little as possible. On the contrary, the rich are always looking for new challenges to keep growing. If you believe you can be happy by doing nothing, you are kidding yourself. To feel satisfied, people need constant news.

Learn Emotional Regulation Techniques

Learn to tolerate uncertainty. Uncertainty is an unpleasant feeling for most people. However, it is important to learn to accept that it can sometimes occur over the course of a lifetime. The inability to tolerate uncertainty can lead to a constant state of fear and worry or to rely too much on others. It can prevent you from taking action and carrying out activities that you find rewarding because you fear that you will fail. By learning to gradually accept uncertainty, you will be able to tolerate it.

Keep a journal of what happens to you all day. Write whenever you feel anxious or insecure. Write down what was happening just before you felt a certain sensation. How did you react at the moment? What have you tried?

Rank your uncertainties. For each one there is a series of troubling or uncomfortable things. Try to rank yours. For example, "go to a new restaurant" might be in second position, while "don't plan your holidays in advance" might be in ninth.

Start testing yourself in small, safe situations. Start gradually with the items that are lower on your leader board. For example, you could go to your favorite restaurant, but order something you've never tried before.
Record these experiences in your journal. How did you feel? Has the situation taken the turn you hoped for? If not - it won't always go as you expect, but that's not a problem! - how did you react? Do you think you can react differently in the future?

Try some techniques to calm yourself down. It is important to know a number of relaxation techniques when you are feeling troubled. They may be different for each person, but some how they mitigate certain feelings. Try a few to understand which ones are best suited to your needs.

Try listening to relaxing music. The British Academy of Sound Therapy used science to put together a playlist of the most relaxing songs in the world, including artists such as Marconi Union and Enya.

Engage in something calm and repetitive, like swimming, knitting, rocking in a chair or hammock, or even repeating a mantra.

Keep your sense of touch engaged by petting your dog or cat. In addition to providing you with a way to focus on your senses, regular interaction with a pet has been shown to reduce depression.

Go for a quiet walk, observing the beauty of your surroundings.

Take a warm bath or hot shower. Heat relaxes and calms most people.

Make an appointment with yourself. Go out for dinner to spend a nice evening surrounded by tablecloths, candles and beautiful paintings, all to yourself. Order your favorite dishes and remember that you deserve this kind of pampering.

Try to calm down with touch. People need the affection produced by physical contact to grow healthily. Positive physical contact produces oxytocin, a powerful hormone that improves mood, relieves stress and leads to forging bonds with others. Below, you will find some techniques you can try to relax in emotionally difficult circumstances.

Put a hand on your heart. Feel the warmth of your skin under your hand. Feel the heartbeat, feel the movement of the chest rising and falling as you breathe. Repeat a few positive words as you pay attention to these feelings, such as "I am worthy to be loved" or "I am worth".

Give yourself a hug. Cross your arms across your chest and place your hands on your upper arms. Try to hold yourself. Notice the sensations in your body. Feel the warmth of your hands and the pressure of your arms. Repeat a positive phrase, such as "I love myself".

Hold your face in your hands, as you would a child or loved one. Caress it with your fingers. Feel the warmth of your hands on your face. Speak some kind words to yourself, even repeating them, such as "I'm beautiful. I'm kind."

Learn to "improve the current situation". One way to avoid being overwhelmed by emotion is to counteract the normal immediate reaction to a given circumstance. Look for solutions that give new meaning to what you are experiencing.

To find new meaning, try reframing experiences. For example, you may feel disheartened that you are not appreciated at work and that your boss neglects your efforts. There is no point in trying to "ignore" this frustration. Rather, try to re-code this episode as an experience from which to learn how to deal with unpleasant people - an excellent skill in life.

If you are a believer, your religiosity can also help you find meaning in a certain situation that seems unpleasant at the moment.

Practice meditation. Many studies have shown that meditation, and in particular mindfulness meditation, can relieve anxiety and depression, but also improve the ability to cope with stress. Mindful meditation, when practiced regularly, can also help stabilize emotions. Try taking a class, use an online meditation guide, or learn on your own.

Find a quiet, comfortable place with no distractions. Sit in a hard-backed chair or upright on the floor. Avoid bending over, otherwise you tire your breath.

Focus on a single element of your breath. It could be the sound of air entering your nose, the expansion of your lungs filling with oxygen, or what you feel while taking deep, cleansing breaths. Focus on this element for a few minutes as you breathe deeply.

Expand your attention to include the rest of your body. Notice what you feel through your other senses. Try not to judge or focus too much on a sensation.

Accept every thought and sensation as it manifests itself. Try to take note of everything without making judgments: "I'm having an itchy sensation in my nose. It's a sensation".

If you lower your concentration, bring your attention back to the breath.

The UCLA Mindful Awareness research facility has made available some MP3 files for meditation, downloadable like those of Buddha Net. There are also many applications available for mobile or tablet that offer guided mini-meditations.

Try other awareness techniques. The fundamental principle of awareness is to accept the experience of the present moment, without resisting or judging it. Of course, this is easier said than done, but you will find that as you become familiar with the techniques of awareness, it will become a new "habit" that the mind will be able to adopt.

When you have an emotionally strong experience, repeat a few helpful phrases to yourself. You can do this out loud or in mind. Here are some examples:

I don't always feel these feelings. They will pass.

My thoughts and feelings are not facts.

I don't have to act in the wake of emotion.

I'm fine right now, even if the situation isn't the best.

Emotions come and go. In the past I have been able to master them.

Identify what you feel without labeling it as "good" or "bad". For example, if you are angry with yourself, find a moment to acknowledge your feeling: "I think I am angry with myself because I have not eaten healthily, even though I had set a goal of consuming healthier foods. Just one of the thoughts I will have today. "

Speak out that you accept what you feel. By telling yourself to accept whatever emotion you show, you will be able to believe it. Remember that emotions are part of human life. By accepting them, you will be able to manage them in the future.

Seek professional help. Sometimes, you try your best to control your emotionality, and nevertheless, you continue to feel overwhelmed by what you are feeling. The difficulty in managing your emotions is likely to be due to a more serious problem, such as past abuse or trauma, or it may indicate a disorder, such as depression. By working with an accredited mental health professional you will be able to discover the useless patterns that govern your thoughts and reactions to emotions, but also to learn new ways to process what you feel in a useful and healthy way.

It is a fairly common belief that only "crazy" people and people who have suffered love disappointments go to the psychotherapist. These labels are harmful and do not even represent reality. Many people turn to a psychological counselor for a variety of reasons.

Another myth is that you can get help from talking to family or friends. Although social support has its importance, sometimes there are problems that require the intervention of a specialized professional. An experienced counselor or therapist can give advice based on scientific techniques and "outside" observations. She can also help the patient to find out if it is necessary to undergo treatment to combat disorders such as depression or anxiety.

Some people believe that it is enough to "resign" and face emotions alone. It's a pretty damaging idea: sometimes, depression or panic attacks physically debilitate people, preventing them from coping with emotions on their own. By seeking a therapist, you will show that you love and respect yourself so much that you are able to get the help you need.

There are usually several places to find the advice you need. You can speak to your doctor to recommend a professional, contact a mental health center or even contact the ASL psychologist.

Advice
Learn to recognize and anticipate the triggers that cause you to explode.
Think about how you see your reactions over 5 years. Will you be proud that you made it, keeping your dignity intact, or will you look back, remembering that you "fell apart"? Make your choice now.

When you notice that your mood changes, step away from the cause and take deep breaths, pray, think about the actions or words that have troubled you and imagine a different way of dealing with the situation.

Regardless of what you choose to do, it's important to keep taking note of how you feel. Just because you don't react to an emotion doesn't mean it doesn't exist.

Be understanding when something suddenly goes wrong with a person. He probably just had a bad day, or you might have caught it at the wrong time.

If a fear or sadness begins to grow, you can try both psychoanalysis and therapeutic counseling. However, if it turns into something of concern, seek professional help.

Warnings

Emotions must be controlled, but not stifled or denied. In fact, by repressing them there is the risk that they give rise to physical ailments and increase symptoms of a psychological nature.

Many emotional problems are so complex that they require additional professional help from a psychologist, psychotherapist, or social worker.

CHAPTER 6

FORGET ABOUT PAST AND LIVE THE PRESENT

Constantly ruminating on your past or focusing on your future could cause you to lose sight of the present, letting life pass you by quickly, without you being able to enjoy it. If you dwell too much on reflecting on past events or traumas or worrying about your future, you can adopt some systems that can help you live in the present.

Forget Past and Future Concerns

Learn to manage past emotions. Regardless of the severity of the event that continues to disturb you, you should externalize your emotions associated with it before you can move on. There could be some painful experiences, but also some good memories. Displaying repressed emotions can help you leave the past behind and focus on the present.

Share your innermost thoughts with a friend, family member, or therapist.

Try to write down the emotions aroused by past events. You can keep a journal or write a letter to someone who has hurt your feelings (without sending it to them!).

Even if you dwell on good memories, you may lose touch with reality. You would find yourself fantasizing about the past and wishing it all went back to the way it used to be, instead of focusing on improving your present.

Forgive and turn the page. Keeping looking back to find the one responsible for your emotional pain negatively affects your present life. Instead of mulling over those who have hurt you, forgive them. Focus on present events and leave all past guilt and suffering behind. Constantly stirring in pain does not harm the one you hold responsible for your unhappiness and brings you to a stalemate.

If necessary, write a letter to the person concerned or deal with it openly. You don't have to send the letter, but that will help you stop blaming her for past actions and focus on the present and your happiness.

Focus on pleasurable experiences. If sharing your past feelings doesn't work, focus on the positive. You can't change the past or worry about the future, so focus on the positive aspects of the present.

If you think it's difficult, create a point of reference. For example, find an isolated spot in which to spend pleasant moments of relaxation. If you find yourself mulling over your past or worrying about your future, think about the happy moments you spend in this quiet and comfortable place.

Repress your memories. If all attempts fail, try to suppress negative thoughts and emotions. Over time, this strategy can help you get over bad memories that, pushed deep inside, will become less nagging. Imagine closing the doors of the past in reference to sad moments and suffering. Creating a mental image will be useful to you, especially if memories or worries are suffocating.

Some studies have shown that self-control of emotions is useful for getting rid of negative memories and cutting ties with the past. If you continuously adopt this strategy you will no longer be prey to your emotions. Whenever bad memories resurface, push them to the back of your mind and strive to forget and overcome the traumatic episodes.

Overcome your anxieties for the future. Whenever you are assailed by anxiety about the future, remember that you can only change the present. Make a list of things that belong to the present. Think about the book you are reading, how nice it would be to be in Hawaii at this time of the year, or some other image that can distract your mind from negative thoughts about your future. Instead of focusing on what might happen, focus your attention on what you can control.

If this is difficult for you, find visual memories to focus on. Bring a copy of the book you are reading with you, or print a photo of the place where you love to spend your free time the most to observe when you feel the need to release the tension.

It will take some practice to find new ideas that don't feed your worries about future events. Don't give up and you will eventually succeed.

Ask for help. If these methods don't work, you should get someone to help you get over the past, worry less about the future, and focus on the present. Look for a specialist in the area where you live; you can ask your doctor or your family and friends for directions. You may consult with different types of specialists, such as counselors, psychotherapists, psychologists and psychiatrists. They specialize in suggesting coping strategies to help people become more productive and constructive by focusing on the present.

Don't be ashamed to ask for help. Your mental health is very important and you shouldn't feel embarrassed. It is a very common problem and medical specialists are always ready to welcome you and help you.

Manage Previous Trauma

Learn to distinguish a traumatic event from painful memories. The trauma causes psychological and physiological effects similar to anxiety and intense fear, as if it were relived in the present. Bad memories trigger painful emotions like sadness and guilt, but they don't alter your perception of reality, as is the case with acute trauma.

The trauma must be dealt with independently and usually requires the intervention of a specialist.

Sometimes it takes many years for the symptoms of trauma to emerge. You may have nightmares, intrusive thoughts, or be prone to depression, anxiety, phobias or flashbacks due to a traumatic event.

Liberation from a traumatic experience can only happen through a very slow and gradual process, but if you continue to work, the situation will improve.

Ask for help from a support group or a specialist who can implement a targeted individual support intervention. You are the architect of your own healing and growth and it's up to you to decide how and when to heal. Regardless of the therapy you choose, the program should include the following steps:

- self-perception: your recovery is an opportunity to regain control of your life. Although a guide is important, you are solely responsible for your health. If your counselor offers you a suggestion that you don't think is valid or that you don't feel ready to follow, you don't need to listen;

- confirm: your experience may have been dwarfed or sidelined over the years. Your group or your counselor can confirm what happened and how the traumatic event negatively affected your existence;
- interpersonal relationships: the experience of a trauma can lead to isolation. Talking about it with other people and sharing your story with someone who can understand you is useful for starting to nurture relationships and overcome any states of discomfort.

Confide in someone you trust. An integral part of the healing process is talking about what happened. Choose someone patient and kind who is aware of the severity of your trauma. People who respond with phrases like "forget it", "forgive and forget" or "it's not that bad" are not the right ones.

You may need to talk about your trauma more than once, so make sure your interlocutor understands its importance. Getting rid of the weight of an oppressive past is positive, but you will need to come back to the subject several times.

If there is no one in your life to whom you feel particularly close or whom you can trust, ask for help from someone you really like. Ask him to do something fun, and if it works, invite him again in the future. Spending time with this person can help you establish a solid relationship.

Know that the empathic relationship with traumatized people can cause vicarious or indirect traumatization, that is, the perception of the same symptoms as the patient. Don't be offended if your friend can't hear your story every day.

Family and friends are a great place to start, but if you need additional support, psychotherapists are trained to avoid vicarious traumatization.

Make a list of ways to take care of yourself. It may be difficult to focus on finding relief when going through tough times. Make a list of the things that help you feel better and put it in a prominent place. Here are some options:

- dedicate yourself to something creative, such as painting, drawing, woodworking, crochet or other manual activities;
- practice moderate physical activity. It doesn't have to be intense - you could just take a walk around your house. Or try running, swimming, playing a sport, dancing, hiking or anything else that keeps you in training;
- play with the kids or with your dog. The game has a calming effect, which can make you feel better;
- sing in a low voice or with full lungs. Fill your lungs with air and sing out your favorite songs;
- wear your favorite shirt or jewelry that you particularly like.

Be Aware of the Present

Learn to appreciate your surroundings. Stop analyzing your life and letting your mind get stuck in the past. Learn to admire everything you see around you, from the wonders of nature to the works made by man. Make an effort to pay attention to each aspect of your present life.

For example, take a walk and observe your surroundings. If you are outdoors, admire the trees, the earth and the whole landscape. Enjoy the breeze that caresses your skin. If you are indoors, pay attention to the color of the walls, the voices of those around you and the feel of the floor under your feet. This will help you focus on the present.

Slow down the pace. Often people whiz at full speed through life, overwhelmed by the frenzy of everyday life and already projected into the next moment. Push the "Pause" button and enjoy every moment, even if it seems boring. For example, pay attention to the gestures you make while you eat a snack. Grab a bunch of grapes and look at it. Note the shape and size of the berries. Eat one and focus on its flavor, enjoying the sweet sensation it gives you on your tongue.

It is normal not to get excited about anything. If you're doing a project that doesn't appeal to you or have a task you don't particularly enjoy, that's fine. Instead of putting it aside, think about all the actions you take every day and learn to appreciate them.

Change your routine. If you do the same thing the same way every day or at the same time every week, you probably get stuck in the past without realizing it. While routine can be comforting, it can help create a deadlock. Try to change your daily habits - for example, you may find a different way to go to the bus stop or to work.

Even making minor changes can help you escape. Change your eating habits and introduce new words into your lexicon every day. Anything noteworthy daily will help you live in the present, rather than the past or future.

If you don't want or can't change your routine, pay more attention to everyday gestures. Take note of the taste of the cereals you eat every morning or the appearance of the trees on your way to work.

CHAPTER 7

GET RID OF BAD MEMORIES

We all have them, those horrible memories that make us want to hide somewhere to escape the past. If we don't deal with them decisively, bad memories can devour us. Confronting them and expressing them aloud is an effective way to relieve the anxiety they cause. It may take some time, but if you are firmly determined to stop these memories from consuming your mind you will find a way.

Try these methods even if they may seem strange to you. First of all, accept that bad memory: accept yourself and your current life. Shout, punch the wall, or cry if you need to (guys, if something really hurts you, you have the right to let your emotions out and cry!). Let this emotion reach your conscience, assimilate the pain and sadness. Think about it. Bring that memory back and try to analyze it.

Accept the reality. One aspect of grief of any kind is sometimes rejection, the question of whether that particular event really happened.

Stop wishing it didn't happen. For example: if a loved one dies, it may happen to see someone similar from behind and hope that it is that person, even if you know that unfortunately they are no longer there. This is an example of a rejection of reality.

Don't be distracted from absorbing this finding. If necessary close privately. Do not watch the TV. You may have to take a sick day or start your day a little later to not get distracted.

Continue to welcome the emotion that comes from that memory. You will realize when you have truly accepted it. And goes on...

Gather your strength so you can think (or say aloud to emphasize) "This is the emotion that scared me. I tried it and faced it. Now I have to let it go and not fight it anymore". Sigh, take a few deep breaths, and let that emotion go - accept it.

Try to understand how you feel now. If you feel the same way as before, it means you haven't really dealt with your feelings. The only way to defeat bad memories is to face them head on, so try again!

Forgive yourself and others for what happened. Get over the frustration and the memory of humiliation you may have felt.

Live life in a positive way despite the difficult experience. Let the memory stay, don't block it. Let it come when it wants but learn to ignore it.

Tell yourself "This is the past, now I am in the present". I can overcome the negative events of the past, because I have the future. I can do whatever I have to do to keep going.

Things change. You can't spend the rest of your life feeling bad - change is part of life. You won't always feel like you have felt in the past or how you feel now. The time you spend thinking that you will always be sick from these memories is wasted time!

Advice

One way to accept the past is to say: "There is a reason why it happened", "That happened then, now I'm in the present", "I'll keep trying, I'll pass this test!", "Everything will be fine! Everything will work out!", "Easy! I can do it!", "I live in the present: here and now - not in the past or in the future", "The past is past, and tomorrow has not yet arrived".

Do not waste time hating memory people and circumstances of that event but accept the memory because it is part of your character, of "who you are". Welcome the peace that comes from this acceptance.

Do not give up. If you can't climb the mountain you will always find it in front of you.

Sometimes you can have nightmares. Talk to someone about it, and if you usually pray don't ask God to make the bad dreams go away but try to be calm and happy when you go to sleep. Make a prayer of thanks for your friends and for all the things, good and bad.

Warnings

Don't make stupid or extreme gestures to accept an emotion. Don't hate yourself or others. Love yourself so that you can love others too. Even if things seem terrible, don't let yourself be overwhelmed by the rejection of reality. Accept and process it.

CHAPTER 8

EMPTY CHAIR TECHNIQUE

The empty chair technique is one of the most used working tools in Gestalt theory. However, it is not exclusive to this current, it is also used by therapists from other branches of psychology. The disclosure of its use is due to the fact that it has proven to be a very effective tool for addressing certain problems.

"The empty chair" is an emotional technique that can be constituted as a great resource for addressing unresolved issues of the past in consultation. By following the appropriate steps, marked by the therapist, the results can be very positive for personal development and, within this, for the emotional. This is because it allows for emotional contact with an absent situation or person. The peculiarity of this contact is that, in it, the patient remains in control at all times.

This technique was devised by Fritz Perls, neuropsychiatrist and psychoanalyst, creator of Gestalt Therapy. He used it when he offered short demonstration sessions to a large audience of professionals who wanted to learn about the Gestalt approach.

However, Jacob Levy Moreno, founder of psychodrama, is also coined for the creation of the empty chair technique. Current in which the use of this tool is also quite frequent. In both currents the use of the technique is the same and has its indications.

What Is the Empty Chair Technique?

The empty chair technique transforms a psychotherapy session into an experiential encounter of the patient. In addition to the usual two chairs used in the psychotherapy set, a third chair is added - the empty chair - in which the person is led to imagine that someone or something is sitting there, and then to talk to them as if they were actually present.

Initially, the person projects into the imagination of the empty chair a part of her personality, an absent person, a feeling or a situation with which he/she has a conflict to open a dialogue. Next, the person, following the therapist's slogan, will move to occupy the role of replacing the empty chair. Dialogue is established through the change of roles in the chair.

That is, the person at first will face what he is projecting on the chair, talk to you and say everything you need as if you were really present in the session. Subsequently, he will take the place of what is imagined and give you the voice that will be addressed to your person.

What aspects does the empty chair technique deal with?
The confrontation that occurs in the staging of the empty chair allows the person to deal with conflicts, both current and past. The idea is to produce an important cathartic and transforming effect. It is usually used for the work of three different purposes.

A Situation or an Event

They work with any event that has significantly affected the person and altered their life in some way. It can represent a disturbing situation or a traumatic event. For example, a rape, an accident, an abuse, a physical assault, or a childhood scene with your mother.

In this way, the person can give a voice and a different understanding in the present to an event that happened in the past. Where, despite what cannot be changed, what happened, through contact with the emotions and thoughts of that moment the person will be able to express what he could not at that moment and give a different meaning to the fact.

The empty chair technique, producing a screen effect - where the person locates their attention and projects the event - can put the person in touch with emotions and how they affect their lives. It gives a different meaning to the way you feel it, if it is in the past and if it is in the present, you discover new ways to deal with and respond to such a situation.

One Person Not Available

The empty chair technique allows working with the evocation of a person with whom there is unfinished business, but is not available at this time, because he is dead, disappeared, abandoned, separated or simply because any other circumstance prevents the meeting.

Using the imagination the person evokes that significant figure - which no longer exists in physical reality, but in his psychological reality - sitting in the empty chair. Once this goal has been achieved, the person turns directly to that figure who occupies the chair, transmitting in the present all the emotions that made him feel in the past and in the present. Recall that the goal is to achieve a cathartic effect.

An Aspect of One's Personality

The person projects aspects of their personality, needs, disabilities, feelings, etc. onto the chair. Being able to manage and better understand the subjective - internal - aspects in a different reality, the concrete reality. By projecting these aspects onto the empty chair, they become more tangible. Somehow it's like they come alive.

When the person projects aspects of his personality into the empty chair, he allows himself to look and examine himself from a distance, from the outside. In this way, he acquires the possibility of obtaining a more impartial impression of himself. Sometimes denying aspects of one's personality is found in the struggle between the person's desire and moral containment, which leads to non-acceptance of oneself.

Use of the Empty Chair Technique

The empty chair technique wants to be a tool through which the person can stage a series of roles to project and obtain cathartic effects. In this sense, you can project into it those aspects of his personality that are not accepted as of him, an absent person, a feeling or a situation with which he has a conflict. All with the aim of integrating them.

Although it is a useful tool that appears to be a simple application, it should be used under the supervision of a therapist. The use of it is intermittent, it cannot be done in all sessions, nor is it recommended for all people. Hence the importance as it is always applied by a therapist.

CHAPTER 9

EMOTIONS AND EMOTIONAL INTELLIGENCE OF LEADER

A Leader, with his attitude and actions, guides and influences the people around him and emotions play a fundamental role. In reality, each of us influences the others, we are all leaders in one way or another: just think of parents, teachers, coaches, craftsmen, managers, entrepreneurs.

What we show on the outside is what we have inside, and the ability to know how to experience positive and strong emotions can make the difference. In this sense, the greatness of a leader is based on the ability to leverage emotions, his own and those of others, to act as a travel companion who does not have the monopoly of truth, but is aware of the responsibility of being the guide of the main resources of every reality, people.

Emotional Intelligence

Emotional intelligence is defined as the ability to appropriately recognize, identify and manage one's own emotions and those of others to achieve certain goals. This concept was theorized only recently, in 1990, by the

American psychologists P. Solovey and J. D. Mayer, subsequently deepened by the psychologist and science journalist Daniel Goleman. According to the latter, emotional intelligence is a fundamental aspect for success in the field of business and leadership.

The 5 pillars on which it is based are self-awareness, motivation, empathy, social skills (communication, leadership, problem solving, decision making) and self-control.

In this direction it is essential:

- the ability to motivate oneself and others and continue to pursue the goal despite difficulties and mistakes;
- controlling impulses despite adverse events;
- modulate one's moods, avoiding that negative emotions prevent us from having quality thoughts;
- cultivate empathy, hope and trust in one's own possibilities and those of collaborators.

Emotional intelligence enables the leader to make optimal decisions, being fully aware both rationally and emotionally, aligned and consistent with his own values and the organization, capable of positively involving others by creating a shared vision.

The Emotional Leader

A good charismatic leader with good communication skills can only be a person with a high emotional, empathic and sensitive IQ.

To be a good leader, excellent technical skills and not even a very high IQ (Intelligence Quotient) are not enough, it is also necessary to have an irrational component, called IE

(Emotional Intelligence), that is a mix of the ability to know and control oneself, to understand and involve others.

The art of leadership is hitting goals through the quality of the work of others, bringing and maintaining them in the highest range of performance levels, and this happens when people are in the best state of personal well-being. The characteristics of this state are: total focus on the action plan to achieve the goal, flexibility and speed of maneuver, process of continuous improvement of personal skills, continuous improvement feedback.

You are an emotional leader when you know how to guide them without necessarily having all the answers and you know how to listen, apologize if you're wrong. When you don't use your role to feel important, but you demonstrate it day after day, getting as close as you can to the figure of the "natural leader".

Emotional Intelligence Is Essential for Leadership

Emotional intelligence is essential because:
- emotions drive people and people drive performance;
- helps in "people management";
- develops motivation and team spirit;
- helps to be focused;
- improves effective relationships;
- creates a positive, stress-free climate;
- increases the work-life balance;
- favors "change management";
- develops optimism.

Emotional Intelligence Can Be Trained

Emotional intelligence can be trained and improved at any age, but the ideal is to start small.

In Denmark, empathy is taught in schools, where children expose their problems and listen to each other without judging each other. Then we analyze the problem and try to solve it together by looking at it "with several eyes", from different perspectives.

However, it is essential to consider that before being taught at school, it must be learned within one's family thanks to parents who show interest in children's emotions.

CHAPTER 10

INTELLIGENCE AND WELL-BEING

Intelligence, what is it? Generally, the cognitive abilities of language and logical reasoning are associated with intelligence. Sometimes the ability to memorize and think in images is also considered.

Compared to the many other skills that the human being has, this vision of intelligence seems to be rather limited - and limiting. Thus, to broaden our mental horizon, it may be useful to look at the etymology of the word "intelligence".

Etymology
The word intelligence derives from the Latin "intellegere" which for the ancient Romans meant: to notice, to perceive, and also to understand. Thus we see that at the basis of the idea of intelligence there are two components: one passive and one active.

In the conception of the ancient Romans, the idea of "intelligence" has to do with a passive function, which consists in knowing how to make oneself receptive to notice, perceive specific information of reality. Secondly, "intelligence" is the ability to actively do something with what is perceived, understand. That is, giving meaning to what is perceived, giving it an order and transforming it into something useful, constructive and that helps improve people's lives.

If we take into consideration its etymological meaning, the concept of "intelligence" presupposes the ability to use and integrate passive and active skills at the same time. In this sense, "intelligence" is something much broader than common sense today, which identifies only active cognitive abilities as characteristics of intelligence (using words correctly, reasoning in a logical-mathematical sense), leaving out all abilities instead passive and receptive.

In the etymological sense of the term, "intelligence" thus becomes the ability to grasp the different nuances of existence and then give them a sense and a meaning. In this way, beyond words and concepts, emotions, sensations and physical abilities, sounds and music, relationships also fall into the field of intelligence.

Widening the concept of "intelligence" in this way allows us to include non-cognitive human dimensions in the field of "important" experiences so that they can be taken into due consideration with regard to the harmonious development and well-being of people.

To this end, I find the intelligence studies of Howard Gardner relevant, who, through scientific methods of investigation, has managed to bring to the attention of scholars the plurality of human skills, not just cognitive ones.

The Theory of Multiple Intelligences

Howard Gardner is an American psychologist, lecturer and researcher at the prestigious Harvard University, famous for his "theory of multiple intelligences".
Gardner's study method was based on observation. Gardner has studied many people with brain injuries and, in this way, he was able to detect that specific deficits in psychological functioning always correspond to lesions of specific brain areas.

With this procedure Gardner was able to isolate a series of skills or "intelligences". These "intelligences" are relatively independent of each other and represent specific methods of information processing.

Based on his studies, Gardner has identified the following "intelligences":

- Linguistic intelligence.
  It is the ability to use written and spoken language to express oneself effectively. People with high linguistic intelligence show a remarkable ability to use words, to learn new languages and words, to read and write. It cannot be missing: in journalists, writers, lawyers, orators (for example politicians);

- Logical-mathematical intelligence.
  It is the ability to analyze problems logically, to think critically, to use mathematical operations, to reason by cause and effect. It cannot be missing: in scientists, engineers, finance professionals and accountants;

- Visual-spatial intelligence.
  It is the ability to visualize through the mind's eye. For example, it allows you to imagine a three-dimensional object and see it rotate mentally. This type of intelligence also concerns the ability to remember and evaluate the spatial characteristics of real places and objects. It cannot be missing: in architects, in those who professionally drive a means of transport (drivers, pilots, truck drivers), in professional graphic designers, in artists who practice visual arts such as: painters, photographers, sculptors and directors;

- Kinesthetic or procedural intelligence.
  It is the ability to accurately control the movements of one's body and to use concrete objects and tools with skill. It cannot be missing: in athletes, dancers, martial artists, soldiers and construction workers;

- Naturalistic intelligence.
  It is the ability to recognize and appreciate the relationships between beings - living and non-living - that make up the world. It cannot be missing: in

veterinarians, biologists, botanists, astronomers and ecologists;

- Interpersonal intelligence.
  It is the ability to understand other people's intentions, motives and emotions. This intelligence allows you to communicate and empathize effectively with others. It cannot be missing: in salespeople, managers, teachers, doctors, social workers and those who work side by side in a "team";

- Intrapersonal intelligence.
  It is the ability to know how to grasp and make sense of one's emotions, intentions and motivations. It cannot be missingin actors;

- Musical intelligence.
  It has to do with sensitivity to sounds, rhythms, melodies and music in general. People with high musical intelligence are usually in tune and can have perfect pitch, that is, the ability to recognize the pitch of notes without the aid of a reference sound (such as a tuning fork). A good musical intelligence also allows you to sing, play musical instruments and compose. It cannot be missing: in musicians, singers, composers and music producers.

IQ vs EQ: Intelligence Quotient and Emotional Quotient

In his 1996 book "Emotional Intelligence", author Daniel Goleman suggested that EQ may actually be more important than IQ. Why? Some psychologists believe that the standard measures of intelligence (i.e. IQ scores) are too narrow and do not include the full range of human intelligence. Instead, they suggest that the ability to understand and express emotions can play an equal if not more important role in how people fare in life.

What Is the Difference Between IQ and EQ?

Let's start by defining the two terms in order to understand what they mean and how they differ. IQ, or intelligence quotient, is a number derived from a standardized intelligence test. On the original intelligence tests, the scores were calculated by dividing the individual's mental age by his chronological age and multiplying that number by 100. So a child with a mental age of 15 and a chronological age of 10 would have an IQ of 150. Today, scores on most intelligence tests are calculated by comparing the beneficiary's score with dozens of other people of the same age group.

EQ, on the other hand, is a measure of a person's level of emotional intelligence. This refers to a person's ability to perceive, control, evaluate and express emotions. Researchers like John Mayer and Peter Salovey, as well as writers like Daniel Goleman have helped shine a light on emotional intelligence, making it a hot topic in areas ranging from business management to education.

Today, you can buy toys that claim to help strengthen a child's emotional intelligence or enroll your children in programs designed to teach emotional intelligence, often referred to by the acronym SEL, which stands for social and emotional learning skills. In some schools in the United States, social and emotional learning is also a requirement of the curriculum.

Does this mean that one of the two is more important?

At one point in time, IQ was seen as the primary success factor. People with high IQs were hired to be destined for a lifetime of achievement, and researchers debated whether intelligence was a product of genes or the environment. However, some critics began to realize that being gifted with great intelligence offered no guarantee of success in life.

IQ is still recognized as an important element of success, particularly when it comes to academic achievement. People with high IQs typically do well in school, often make more money, and tend to be healthier overall. But today experts recognize that this is not the only factor that determines success in a lifetime. Instead, it is part of a complex series of influences that includes, among other things, emotional intelligence.

The concept of emotional intelligence has had a major impact in a number of sectors, including the business world.

Many companies now require training with an emotional intelligence test as part of the hiring process. Research has found that people with strong potential leadership also tend to be more emotionally intelligent, suggesting that high EQ is an important quality that entrepreneurs and managers should possess.

So one might ask, if emotional intelligence is so important that it can be taught or strengthened? According to a meta-analysis that examined the results of social and emotional learning programs, the answer to this question is an unambiguous yes. The study found that about 50 percent of the teens enrolled in SEL courses had the best signs of achievement and nearly 40 percent showed improvement in mean scores. These programs have also been linked to a spike in suspension rates, an increase in school attendance, and a reduction in disciplinary problems.

Conclusion
Research carried out by the Carnegie Institute of Technology shows that 85 percent of your financial success is due to human engineering skills, your personality and the ability to communicate, negotiate, and lead. Incredibly, only 15 percent is due to technical knowledge. Additionally, Nobel Prize Winning Israeli-American psychologist Daniel Kahneman found that people prefer to do business with someone they like and trust, even if the nice person is offering a lower quality product or service at a lower price.

IQ alone is not enough; EQ is important too. In fact, psychologists agree that among the ingredients for success, IQ counts for about 10 percent (at best 25 percent). Everything else depends on other factors including the EQ.

CHAPTER 11

BE HAPPY WITH YOURSELF

To be happy with yourself, or have a positive identity, you need to learn to appreciate your personal, professional, and social self. Most people, young or adult, of any race or nationality, sometimes feel bad about themselves, a negative feeling that can result from personal, job or social dissatisfaction. To be able to develop a positive identity, the best thing to do is to learn to accept the uniqueness of your qualities and to love yourself for who you are, while making a commitment to pursue your goals (personal, professional and social) and to increase your social connections.

Accept Yourself

Appreciate diversity. Learning to accept yourself is essential if you want to develop a positive identity. In this regard, it is important to keep in mind that every human being is different: in fact, no two faces or two bodies are completely identical throughout the world. But if there are no rules that determine how people should be, how is it possible that there is any form of inferiority? By learning to appreciate the diversity that characterizes the world, you will be able to begin to accept and love yourself more.

Make a list of all the different aspects you appreciate in the world. Here are some possible examples: religion, culture, environment, skin color, talents, personality. These variables are what make all human beings - including yourself - interesting and unique.

Appreciate the uniqueness of your qualities. There is no "normal" human being, and there is no "normal" conformation for a human being.

Accept your differences in a positive way. For example "Wow, I have huge feet, but they are what makes me unique!".

Start viewing mistakes and flaws as opportunities to learn or improve yourself.

Stop considering as flaws those aspects of yourself that you cannot change (skin color, height, etc.), instead classify them as unique qualities that make you yourself. "Inferiority" and imperfections can also be seen as unique or individual qualities: were it not for those details, we could be generic clones without any unique traits.

Avoid comparing yourself to others. Nobody's perfect. It is said that the neighbor's grass is always greener; by focusing on the idea that there will always be someone in the world with more money than you or more beautiful than you, you will have a hard time being happy.

At first glance, other people may appear perfect, but like you everyone has his flaws.

When youare comparing yourself to others, stop immediately and reframe your thoughts. Shift attention to your particularities that you find interesting. Compliment yourself for developing them.

Understand that most people don't intend to judge you. Most of them don't know that you got a bad grade on your last math test or that you gained some weight since last summer.

Forgive yourself. Those who are able to accept themselves have the ability to forgive themselves for their past mistakes and do not allow such incidents to define them as persons. Your history and your mistakes do not determine who you are; it is only your actions in the present moment and the person you decide to be in this moment that defines you.

Consciously admit your mistakes and regrets. Reflect on each individual situation and forgive yourself for the mistakes you've made. You can do this in your mind or out loud, saying for example, "I made a mistake, but I forgive myself. That doesn't make me a bad person. In the future I will choose not to repeat my mistakes."

Also identify your past achievements and positive behaviors. Examples might include: graduating, passing an exam, caring for your personal relationships, accomplishing a goal, or being helpful to someone. These positive events are likely to cloud your mistakes and help you focus on the positive aspects of your past.

Love Yourself

Identify your values. Your personal values have a huge impact on your beliefs, goals and identity. They are what you feel is important in your life and can include things like family, knowledge, kindness, and so on. Identifying your values can help you understand who you are and what is most important to you.

Make a list of times when you felt happiest. What were you doing? Who were you with?

So make a list of the moments you felt most proud of. What was the cause of this feeling? Were the others proud too? Who?

Make a list of the times you felt most satisfied. Were they experiences that gave your life more meaning? Such as which ones? Why? Was it the gratification of a particular desire? Which?

Review your lists and try to identify what values those experiences represent. Examples may include: growth, faith, determination, passion, love, loyalty, patriotism, honor, intellect, generosity, etc. You could use this list as a reference or search online for examples of personal values.

Finally, go back to the values you managed to identify and try to determine which of these are the three most important to you.

The first step in learning to love yourself is to commit to getting to know yourself better. Athletes who are able to love each other tend to have more positive emotions and have a higher esteem for themselves and their behaviors. Part of loving yourself is to truly understand who you are or to create your own identity. The parts that make up your identity define who you are.

List the most important aspects of your identity. Here are some examples: athlete, mother, child, granddaughter, passionate person, dancer, writer, etc. Each is an important identity that you can learn to love and appreciate.

Think positively about yourself. How you think about yourself affects your feelings and behaviors. Overall, evaluating your identity in positive terms can help you feel happier about yourself.

Stop and think about your strengths (everyone has them): you will find that you feel happier and more confident about yourself! Look on the bright side of everything!

Create positive mental images. Using your imagination helps you develop greater self-confidence. Imagine that you are totally confident and happy with who you are. How does it feel? What is happening? How did you do it?

Use positive internal dialogue. Positive affirmations help you develop greater self-confidence and reduce negative emotions, such as anxiety.

If you feel bad about yourself, try to make positive statements, such as: "It doesn't matter if I didn't get the grade I wanted, it doesn't make me a bad student. I know I'm a great student, I just need to understand how. I can do better next time, everything will be fine ". The key is to not allow small mistakes to become part of your overall identity. Don't allow yourself to believe that hardships make you a bad person.

Respect yourself. Respecting yourself means treating yourself well and expecting others to do the same.
Take care of yourself physically and mentally. Poor health can seriously jeopardize your overall well-being.
Establish boundaries between yourself and others. For example, don't allow someone to undermine your self-esteem by making fun of an aspect of you that you struggle to accept. If you feel particularly sensitive about your body weight, avoid joking about it, otherwise others may feel empowered to do the same.

Develop your character. Having virtuous qualities, such as wisdom, courage, humanity, and a sense of justice or proportion, can help you form a positive identity.
If you want to focus more on helping others, you can donate some of your money or time (by volunteering) to a charity of your choice. This way you will have the feeling that you are more useful for your community or for the whole world.

Set yourself positive and achievable goals. Focus on correcting those aspects of you and your life that you can change. Having goals and making a commitment to achieve them can help you feel happier about yourself. By doing so you will gradually get closer to your ideal self.

Find a job. Not feeling good about yourself could be linked to the lack of a job. Stop focusing on the things you can't change. There are some things you can manage to get (a job, lose weight...), while others are not achievable. Aspects like height, ethnicity and upbringing are very difficult to change in a healthy way. So learn to manage them and accept them as they are.

Engage in activities that allow you to express yourself. They could help you feel more motivated and happier overall. To be able to achieve your goals it is important to have a high internal motivation, because it makes you able to self-encourage yourself rather than having to rely on external recognition (in terms of praise or financial gains).
Activities that allow you to express yourself can include those that make you feel alive, complete and involved, and all those that you think you are particularly predisposed to, suitable for, and that allow you to be the real you.

Determine your purpose. What do you want to be remembered for? For being a good parent or friend, or perhaps for helping others?
Be consistent. Never give up. Don't give up on opportunities for fear of making mistakes.

Increase Social Connections

Be sociable. Lack of interpersonal relationships can seriously jeopardize your well-being. Don't be too focused on yourself; be interested in other people's lives.
Find the right balance between your personal and social identity. You can do this by being spontaneous and honest.

Be yourself and don't impersonate a false identity.
Celebrate your achievements with others. Doing so can create a sense of shared happiness. Celebrate your accomplishments, such as a new job, promotion, good grade, new home, engagement, wedding, etc.

Surround yourself with positive people who are eager to support you. Receiving the support of others is an important component of the process that will lead you to feel happy with yourself. To strengthen ourselves and to believe in us, we need to be surrounded by people.
Whenever you spot the presence of a negative person, who puts you in a bad mood or who treats you in a rude way, you will have to stop and think and decide if it is worth keeping your relationship alive.

Ask a friend for help. Good friends help you achieve your goals, whatever they are. They always know how to be honest, and together you can find ways to make youfeel better about yourself.
Talk to a friend about aspects of yourself that don't suit you.

If you have trouble confiding in a friend, ask him if he has ever felt inadequate or unhappy with himself - you may be surprised to hear his response.

Inspire and help others. It stimulates people to give their best - a virtuous quality that can help you develop your positive identity. By having the ability to radiate positivity and happiness, you will be able to internalize those same emotions.

When you find yourself looking for a compliment, back off! Whenever you notice that a person has a cool haircut or is wearing a nice shirt, let them know! In addition to helping him/her feel better about himself/herself, you will also feel happier.

CPSIA information can be obtained
at www.ICGtesting.com
Printed in the USA
BVHW062330220321
603180BV00003B/343